08

ISBN 0-8373-0629-9

C-629   CAREER EXAMINATION SERIES

This is your
PASSBOOK® for...

D1373689

Public
Health
Assistant

Test Preparation Study Guide

Questions & Answers

NLC

NATIONAL LEARNING CORPORATION

PASSBOOK®

NOTICE

This book is *SOLELY* intended for, is sold *ONLY* to, and its use is *RESTRICTED* to *individual*, bona fide applicants or candidates who qualify by virtue of having seriously filed applications for appropriate license, certificate, professional and/or promotional advancement, higher school matriculation, scholarship, or other legitimate requirements of educational and/or governmental authorities.

This book is *NOT* intended for use, class instruction, tutoring, training, duplication, copying, reprinting, excerption, or adaptation, etc., by:

(1) Other Publishers

(2) Proprietors and/or Instructors of "Coaching" and/or Preparatory Courses

(3) Personnel and/or Training Divisions of commercial, industrial, and governmental organizations

(4) Schools, colleges, or universities and/or their departments and staffs, including teachers and other personnel

(5) Testing Agencies or Bureaus

(6) Study groups which seek by the purchase of a single volume to copy and/or duplicate and/or adapt this material for use by the group as a whole without having purchased individual volumes for each of the members of the group

(7) Et al.

Such persons would be in violation of appropriate Federal and State statutes.

PROVISION OF LICENSING AGREEMENTS. — Recognized educational commercial, industrial, and governmental institutions and organizations, and others legitimately engaged in educational pursuits, including training, testing, and measurement activities, may address a request for a licensing agreement to the copyright owners, who will determine whether, and under what conditions, including fees and charges, the materials in this book may be used by them. In other words, a licensing facility *exists* for the legitimate use of the material in this book on other than an individual basis. However, it is asseverated and affirmed here that the materials in this book *CANNOT* be used without the receipt of the express permission of such a licensing agreement from the Publishers.

NATIONAL LEARNING CORPORATION
212 Michael Drive
Syosset, New York 11791

Inquiries re licensing agreements should be addressed to:
The President
National Learning Corporation
212 Michael Drive
Syosset, New York 11791

PASSBOOK SERIES®

THE *PASSBOOK SERIES®* has been created to prepare applicants and candidates for the ultimate academic battlefield – the examination room.

At some time in our lives, each and every one of us may be required to take an examination – for validation, matriculation, admission, qualification, registration, certification, or licensure.

Based on the assumption that every applicant or candidate has met the basic formal educational standards, has taken the required number of courses, and read the necessary texts, the *PASSBOOK SERIES®* furnishes the one special preparation which may assure passing with confidence, instead of failing with insecurity. Examination questions – together with answers – are furnished as the basic vehicle for study so that the mysteries of the examination and its compounding difficulties may be eliminated or diminished by a sure method.

This book is meant to help you pass your examination provided that you qualify and are serious in your objective.

The entire field is reviewed through the huge store of content information which is succinctly presented through a provocative and challenging approach – the question-and-answer method.

A climate of success is established by furnishing the correct answers at the end of each test.

You soon learn to recognize types of questions, forms of questions, and patterns of questioning. You may even begin to anticipate expected outcomes.

You perceive that many questions are repeated or adapted so that you can gain acute insights, which may enable you to score many sure points.

You learn how to confront new questions, or types of questions, and to attack them confidently and work out the correct answers.

You note objectives and emphases, and recognize pitfalls and dangers, so that you may make positive educational adjustments.

Moreover, you are kept fully informed in relation to new concepts, methods, practices, and directions in the field.

You discover that you are actually taking the examination all the time: you are preparing for the examination by "taking" an examination, not by reading extraneous and/or supererogatory textbooks.

In short, this PASSBOOK®, used directedly, should be an important factor in helping you to pass your test.

PUBLIC HEALTH ASSISTANT

JOB DESCRIPTION
Under direct supervision, assists medical and/or professional staff in schools and public health clinics by performing clerical and health-related duties; performs related work.

EXAMPLES OF TYPICAL TASKS
Performs vision, hearing and simple urinalysis tests; weighs and measures patients; takes pulse, respiration rates and temperatures; collects specimens; prepares patients for examination and assists professional staff during examination; operates related equipment; may administer simple first aid; interviews clients to obtain identifying and routine medical information; explains testing and clinic procedures to clients; answers routine questions and makes appropriate referrals; makes and receives related telephone calls; comforts patients, reports relevant observations and information to the professional staff; may accompany nurse on home visits; organizes, maintains, retrieves and replaces medical folders, charts and forms; reviews for completeness, and records and transcribes medical information onto appropriate forms, documents, and charts; labels specimens; serves as a receptionist, schedules medical appointments; and contacts patients via telephone or mail regarding appointsments; sends, receives and sorts mail, medical records and notices; collects and records statistical data; maintains logs and schedules; requests, arranges and maintains equipment and supplies; does light housekeeping and cleaning of instruments and equipment.

TESTS
The written test may include questions concerning record keeping and office procedures, knowledge of terms and equipment used in clinics or other health centers, judgment, ability to follow directions, sanitation and storing methods, and related matters.

HOW TO TAKE A TEST

I. YOU MUST PASS AN EXAMINATION

A. WHAT EVERY CANDIDATE SHOULD KNOW

Examination applicants often ask us for help in preparing for the written test. What can I study in advance? What kinds of questions will be asked? How will the test be given? How will the papers be graded?

As an applicant for a civil service examination, you may be wondering about some of these things. Our purpose here is to suggest effective methods of advance study and to describe civil service examinations.

Your chances for success on this examination can be increased if you know how to prepare. Those "pre-examination jitters" can be reduced if you know what to expect. You can even experience an adventure in good citizenship if you know why civil service exams are given.

B. WHY ARE CIVIL SERVICE EXAMINATIONS GIVEN?

Civil service examinations are important to you in two ways. As a citizen, you want public jobs filled by employees who know how to do their work. As a job seeker, you want a fair chance to compete for that job on an equal footing with other candidates. The best-known means of accomplishing this two-fold goal is the competitive examination.

Exams are widely publicized throughout the nation. They may be administered for jobs in federal, state, city, municipal, town or village governments or agencies.

Any citizen may apply, with some limitations, such as the age or residence of applicants. Your experience and education may be reviewed to see whether you meet the requirements for the particular examination. When these requirements exist, they are reasonable and applied consistently to all applicants. Thus, a competitive examination may cause you some uneasiness now, but it is your privilege and safeguard.

C. HOW ARE CIVIL SERVICE EXAMS DEVELOPED?

Examinations are carefully written by trained technicians who are specialists in the field known as "psychological measurement," in consultation with recognized authorities in the field of work that the test will cover. These experts recommend the subject matter areas or skills to be tested; only those knowledges or skills important to your success on the job are included. The most reliable books and source materials available are used as references. Together, the experts and technicians judge the difficulty level of the questions.

Test technicians know how to phrase questions so that the problem is clearly stated. Their ethics do not permit "trick" or "catch" questions. Questions may have been tried out on sample groups, or subjected to statistical analysis, to determine their usefulness.

Written tests are often used in combination with performance tests, ratings of training and experience, and oral interviews. All of these measures combine to form the best-known means of finding the right person for the right job.

II. HOW TO PASS THE WRITTEN TEST

A. NATURE OF THE EXAMINATION

To prepare intelligently for civil service examinations, you should know how they differ from school examinations you have taken. In school you were assigned certain definite pages to read or subjects to cover. The examination questions were quite detailed and usually emphasized memory. Civil service exams, on the other hand, try to discover your present ability to perform the duties of a position, plus your potentiality to learn these duties. In other words, a civil service exam attempts to predict how successful you will be. Questions cover such a broad area that they cannot be as minute and detailed as school exam questions.

In the public service similar kinds of work, or positions, are grouped together in one "class." This process is known as *position-classification*. All the positions in a class are paid according to the salary range for that class. One class title covers all of these positions, and they are all tested by the same examination.

B. FOUR BASIC STEPS

1) Study the announcement

How, then, can you know what subjects to study? Our best answer is: "Learn as much as possible about the class of positions for which you've applied." The exam will test the knowledge, skills and abilities needed to do the work.

Your most valuable source of information about the position you want is the official exam announcement. This announcement lists the training and experience qualifications. Check these standards and apply only if you come reasonably close to meeting them.

The brief description of the position in the examination announcement offers some clues to the subjects which will be tested. Think about the job itself. Review the duties in your mind. Can you perform them, or are there some in which you are rusty? Fill in the blank spots in your preparation.

Many jurisdictions preview the written test in the exam announcement by including a section called "Knowledge and Abilities Required," "Scope of the Examination," or some similar heading. Here you will find out specifically what fields will be tested.

2) Review your own background

Once you learn in general what the position is all about, and what you need to know to do the work, ask yourself which subjects you already know fairly well and which need improvement. You may wonder whether to concentrate on improving your strong areas or on building some background in your fields of weakness. When the announcement has specified "some knowledge" or "considerable knowledge," or has used adjectives like "beginning principles of..." or "advanced ... methods," you can get a clue as to the number and difficulty of questions to be asked in any given field. More questions, and hence broader coverage, would be included for those subjects which are more important in the work. Now weigh your strengths and weaknesses against the job requirements and prepare accordingly.

3) Determine the level of the position

Another way to tell how intensively you should prepare is to understand the level of the job for which you are applying. Is it the entering level? In other words, is this the position in which beginners in a field of work are hired? Or is it an intermediate or advanced level? Sometimes this is indicated by such words as "Junior" or "Senior" in the class title. Other jurisdictions use Roman numerals to designate the level – Clerk I, Clerk II, for example. The word "Supervisor" sometimes appears in the title. If the level is not indicated by the title, check the description of duties. Will you be working under very close supervision, or will you have responsibility for independent decisions in this work?

4) Choose appropriate study materials

Now that you know the subjects to be examined and the relative amount of each subject to be covered, you can choose suitable study materials. For beginning level jobs, or even advanced ones, if you have a pronounced weakness in some aspect of your training, read a modern, standard textbook in that field. Be sure it is up to date and has general coverage. Such books are normally available at your library, and the librarian will be glad to help you locate one. For entry-level positions, questions of appropriate difficulty are chosen – neither highly advanced questions, nor those too simple. Such questions require careful thought but not advanced training.

If the position for which you are applying is technical or advanced, you will read more advanced, specialized material. If you are already familiar with the basic principles of your field, elementary textbooks would waste your time. Concentrate on advanced textbooks and technical periodicals. Think through the concepts and review difficult problems in your field.

These are all general sources. You can get more ideas on your own initiative, following these leads. For example, training manuals and publications of the government agency which employs workers in your field can be useful, particularly for technical and professional positions. A letter or visit to the government department involved may result in more specific study suggestions, and certainly will provide you with a more definite idea of the exact nature of the position you are seeking.

III. KINDS OF TESTS

Tests are used for purposes other than measuring knowledge and ability to perform specified duties. For some positions, it is equally important to test ability to make adjustments to new situations or to profit from training. In others, basic mental abilities not dependent on information are essential. Questions which test these things may not appear as pertinent to the duties of the position as those which test for knowledge and information. Yet they are often highly important parts of a fair examination. For very general questions, it is almost impossible to help you direct your study efforts. What we can do is to point out some of the more common of these general abilities needed in public service positions and describe some typical questions.

1) General information

Broad, general information has been found useful for predicting job success in some kinds of work. This is tested in a variety of ways, from vocabulary lists to questions about current events. Basic background in some field of work, such as sociology or economics, may be sampled in a group of questions. Often these are principles which have become familiar to most persons through exposure rather than through formal training. It is difficult to advise you how to study for these questions; being alert to the world around you is our best suggestion.

2) Verbal ability

An example of an ability needed in many positions is verbal or language ability. Verbal ability is, in brief, the ability to use and understand words. Vocabulary and grammar tests are typical measures of this ability. Reading comprehension or paragraph interpretation questions are common in many kinds of civil service tests. You are given a paragraph of written material and asked to find its central meaning.

3) Numerical ability

Number skills can be tested by the familiar arithmetic problem, by checking paired lists of numbers to see which are alike and which are different, or by interpreting charts and graphs. In the latter test, a graph may be printed in the test booklet which you are asked to use as the basis for answering questions.

4) Observation

A popular test for law-enforcement positions is the observation test. A picture is shown to you for several minutes, then taken away. Questions about the picture test your ability to observe both details and larger elements.

5) Following directions

In many positions in the public service, the employee must be able to carry out written instructions dependably and accurately. You may be given a chart with several columns, each column listing a variety of information. The questions require you to carry out directions involving the information given in the chart.

6) Skills and aptitudes

Performance tests effectively measure some manual skills and aptitudes. When the skill is one in which you are trained, such as typing or shorthand, you can practice. These tests are often very much like those given in business school or high school courses. For many of the other skills and aptitudes, however, no short-time preparation can be made. Skills and abilities natural to you or that you have developed throughout your lifetime are being tested.

Many of the general questions just described provide all the data needed to answer the questions and ask you to use your reasoning ability to find the answers. Your best preparation for these tests, as well as for tests of facts and ideas, is to be at your physical and mental best. You, no doubt, have your own methods of getting into an exam-taking mood and keeping "in shape." The next section lists some ideas on this subject.

IV. KINDS OF QUESTIONS

Only rarely is the "essay" question, which you answer in narrative form, used in civil service tests. Civil service tests are usually of the short-answer type. Full instructions for answering these questions will be given to you at the examination. But in case this is your first experience with short-answer questions and separate answer sheets, here is what you need to know:

1) Multiple-choice Questions

Most popular of the short-answer questions is the "multiple choice" or "best answer" question. It can be used, for example, to test for factual knowledge, ability to solve problems or judgment in meeting situations found at work.

A multiple-choice question is normally one of three types—

- It can begin with an incomplete statement followed by several possible endings. You are to find the one ending which *best* completes the statement, although some of the others may not be entirely wrong.
- It can also be a complete statement in the form of a question which is answered by choosing one of the statements listed.
- It can be in the form of a problem – again you select the best answer.

Here is an example of a multiple-choice question with a discussion which should give you some clues as to the method for choosing the right answer:

When an employee has a complaint about his assignment, the action which will *best* help him overcome his difficulty is to
- A. discuss his difficulty with his coworkers
- B. take the problem to the head of the organization
- C. take the problem to the person who gave him the assignment
- D. say nothing to anyone about his complaint

In answering this question, you should study each of the choices to find which is best. Consider choice "A" – Certainly an employee may discuss his complaint with fellow employees, but no change or improvement can result, and the complaint remains unresolved. Choice "B" is a poor choice since the head of the organization probably does not know what assignment you have been given, and taking your problem to him is known as "going over the head" of the supervisor. The supervisor, or person who made the assignment, is the person who can clarify it or correct any injustice. Choice "C" is, therefore, correct. To say nothing, as in choice "D," is unwise. Supervisors have and interest in knowing the problems employees are facing, and the employee is seeking a solution to his problem.

2) True/False Questions

The "true/false" or "right/wrong" form of question is sometimes used. Here a complete statement is given. Your job is to decide whether the statement is right or wrong.

SAMPLE: A person-to-person long-distance telephone call costs less than a station-to-station call to the same city.

This statement is wrong, or false, since person-to-person calls are more expensive.

This is not a complete list of all possible question forms, although most of the others are variations of these common types. You will always get complete directions for answering questions. Be sure you understand *how* to mark your answers – ask questions until you do.

V. RECORDING YOUR ANSWERS

For an examination with very few applicants, you may be told to record your answers in the test booklet itself. Separate answer sheets are much more common. If this separate answer sheet is to be scored by machine – and this is often the case – it is highly important that you mark your answers correctly in order to get credit.

An electric scoring machine is often used in civil service offices because of the speed with which papers can be scored. Machine-scored answer sheets must be marked with a pencil, which will be given to you. This pencil has a high graphite content which responds to the electric scoring machine. As a matter of fact, stray dots may register as answers, so do not let your pencil rest on the answer sheet while you are pondering the correct answer. Also, if your pencil lead breaks or is otherwise defective, ask for another.

Since the answer sheet will be dropped in a slot in the scoring machine, be careful not to bend the corners or get the paper crumpled.

The answer sheet normally has five vertical columns of numbers, with 30 numbers to a column. These numbers correspond to the question numbers in your test booklet. After each number, going across the page are four or five pairs of dotted lines. These short dotted lines have small letters or numbers above them. The first two pairs may also have a "T" or "F" above the letters. This indicates that the first two pairs only are to be used if the questions are of the true-false type. If the questions are multiple choice, disregard the "T" and "F" and pay attention only to the small letters or numbers.

Answer your questions in the manner of the sample that follows:

32. The largest city in the United States is
    A. Washington, D.C.
    B. New York City
    C. Chicago
    D. Detroit
    E. San Francisco

1) Choose the answer you think is best. (New York City is the largest, so "B" is correct.)
2) Find the row of dotted lines numbered the same as the question you are answering. (Find row number 32)
3) Find the pair of dotted lines corresponding to the answer. (Find the pair of lines under the mark "B.")
4) Make a solid black mark between the dotted lines.

VI. BEFORE THE TEST

Common sense will help you find procedures to follow to get ready for an examination. Too many of us, however, overlook these sensible measures. Indeed, nervousness and fatigue have been found to be the most serious reasons why applicants fail to do their best on civil service tests. Here is a list of reminders:

- Begin your preparation early – Don't wait until the last minute to go scurrying around for books and materials or to find out what the position is all about.
- Prepare continuously – An hour a night for a week is better than an all-night cram session. This has been definitely established. What is more, a night a

week for a month will return better dividends than crowding your study into a shorter period of time.

- Locate the place of the exam – You have been sent a notice telling you when and where to report for the examination. If the location is in a different town or otherwise unfamiliar to you, it would be well to inquire the best route and learn something about the building.
- Relax the night before the test – Allow your mind to rest. Do not study at all that night. Plan some mild recreation or diversion; then go to bed early and get a good night's sleep.
- Get up early enough to make a leisurely trip to the place for the test – This way unforeseen events, traffic snarls, unfamiliar buildings, etc. will not upset you.
- Dress comfortably – A written test is not a fashion show. You will be known by number and not by name, so wear something comfortable.
- Leave excess paraphernalia at home – Shopping bags and odd bundles will get in your way. You need bring only the items mentioned in the official notice you received; usually everything you need is provided. Do not bring reference books to the exam. They will only confuse those last minutes and be taken away from you when in the test room.
- Arrive somewhat ahead of time – If because of transportation schedules you must get there very early, bring a newspaper or magazine to take your mind off yourself while waiting.
- Locate the examination room – When you have found the proper room, you will be directed to the seat or part of the room where you will sit. Sometimes you are given a sheet of instructions to read while you are waiting. Do not fill out any forms until you are told to do so; just read them and be prepared.
- Relax and prepare to listen to the instructions
- If you have any physical problem that may keep you from doing your best, be sure to tell the test administrator. If you are sick or in poor health, you really cannot do your best on the exam. You can come back and take the test some other time.

VII. AT THE TEST

The day of the test is here and you have the test booklet in your hand. The temptation to get going is very strong. Caution! There is more to success than knowing the right answers. You must know how to identify your papers and understand variations in the type of short-answer question used in this particular examination. Follow these suggestions for maximum results from your efforts:

1) Cooperate with the monitor
The test administrator has a duty to create a situation in which you can be as much at ease as possible. He will give instructions, tell you when to begin, check to see that you are marking your answer sheet correctly, and so on. He is not there to guard you, although he will see that your competitors do not take unfair advantage. He wants to help you do your best.

2) Listen to all instructions
Don't jump the gun! Wait until you understand all directions. In most civil service tests you get more time than you need to answer the questions. So don't be in a hurry.

Read each word of instructions until you clearly understand the meaning. Study the examples, listen to all announcements and follow directions. Ask questions if you do not understand what to do.

3) Identify your papers

Civil service exams are usually identified by number only. You will be assigned a number; you must not put your name on your test papers. Be sure to copy your number correctly. Since more than one exam may be given, copy your exact examination title.

4) Plan your time

Unless you are told that a test is a "speed" or "rate of work" test, speed itself is usually not important. Time enough to answer all the questions will be provided, but this does not mean that you have all day. An overall time limit has been set. Divide the total time (in minutes) by the number of questions to determine the approximate time you have for each question.

5) Do not linger over difficult questions

If you come across a difficult question, mark it with a paper clip (useful to have along) and come back to it when you have been through the booklet. One caution if you do this – be sure to skip a number on your answer sheet as well. Check often to be sure that you have not lost your place and that you are marking in the row numbered the same as the question you are answering.

6) Read the questions

Be sure you know what the question asks! Many capable people are unsuccessful because they failed to *read* the questions correctly.

7) Answer all questions

Unless you have been instructed that a penalty will be deducted for incorrect answers, it is better to guess than to omit a question.

8) Speed tests

It is often better NOT to guess on speed tests. It has been found that on timed tests people are tempted to spend the last few seconds before time is called in marking answers at random – without even reading them – in the hope of picking up a few extra points. To discourage this practice, the instructions may warn you that your score will be "corrected" for guessing. That is, a penalty will be applied. The incorrect answers will be deducted from the correct ones, or some other penalty formula will be used.

9) Review your answers

If you finish before time is called, go back to the questions you guessed or omitted to give them further thought. Review other answers if you have time.

10) Return your test materials

If you are ready to leave before others have finished or time is called, take ALL your materials to the monitor and leave quietly. Never take any test material with you. The monitor can discover whose papers are not complete, and taking a test booklet may be grounds for disqualification.

VIII. EXAMINATION TECHNIQUES

1) Read the general instructions carefully. These are usually printed on the first page of the exam booklet. As a rule, these instructions refer to the timing of the examination; the fact that you should not start work until the signal and must stop work at a signal, etc. If there are any *special* instructions, such as a choice of questions to be answered, make sure that you note this instruction carefully.

2) When you are ready to start work on the examination, that is as soon as the signal has been given, read the instructions to each question booklet, underline any key words or phrases, such as *least*, *best*, *outline*, *describe* and the like. In this way you will tend to answer as requested rather than discover on reviewing your paper that you *listed without describing*, that you selected the *worst* choice rather than the *best* choice, etc.

3) If the examination is of the objective or multiple-choice type – that is, each question will also give a series of possible answers: A, B, C or D, and you are called upon to select the best answer and write the letter next to that answer on your answer paper – it is advisable to start answering each question in turn. There may be anywhere from 50 to 100 such questions in the three or four hours allotted and you can see how much time would be taken if you read through all the questions before beginning to answer any. Furthermore, if you come across a question or group of questions which you know would be difficult to answer, it would undoubtedly affect your handling of all the other questions.

4) If the examination is of the essay type and contains but a few questions, it is a moot point as to whether you should read all the questions before starting to answer any one. Of course, if you are given a choice – say five out of seven and the like – then it is essential to read all the questions so you can eliminate the two that are most difficult. If, however, you are asked to answer all the questions, there may be danger in trying to answer the easiest one first because you may find that you will spend too much time on it. The best technique is to answer the first question, then proceed to the second, etc.

5) Time your answers. Before the exam begins, write down the time it started, then add the time allowed for the examination and write down the time it must be completed, then divide the time available somewhat as follows:
   - If 3-1/2 hours are allowed, that would be 210 minutes. If you have 80 objective-type questions, that would be an average of 2-1/2 minutes per question. Allow yourself no more than 2 minutes per question, or a total of 160 minutes, which will permit about 50 minutes to review.
   - If for the time allotment of 210 minutes there are 7 essay questions to answer, that would average about 30 minutes a question. Give yourself only 25 minutes per question so that you have about 35 minutes to review.

6) The most important instruction is to *read each question* and make sure you know what is wanted. The second most important instruction is to *time yourself properly* so that you answer every question. The third most

important instruction is to *answer every question*. Guess if you have to but include something for each question. Remember that you will receive no credit for a blank and will probably receive some credit if you write something in answer to an essay question. If you guess a letter – say "B" for a multiple-choice question – you may have guessed right. If you leave a blank as an answer to a multiple-choice question, the examiners may respect your feelings but it will not add a point to your score. Some exams may penalize you for wrong answers, so in such cases *only*, you may not want to guess unless you have some basis for your answer.

7) Suggestions
   a. Objective-type questions
      1. Examine the question booklet for proper sequence of pages and questions
      2. Read all instructions carefully
      3. Skip any question which seems too difficult; return to it after all other questions have been answered
      4. Apportion your time properly; do not spend too much time on any single question or group of questions
      5. Note and underline key words – *all, most, fewest, least, best, worst, same, opposite,* etc.
      6. Pay particular attention to negatives
      7. Note unusual option, e.g., unduly long, short, complex, different or similar in content to the body of the question
      8. Observe the use of "hedging" words – *probably, may, most likely,* etc.
      9. Make sure that your answer is put next to the same number as the question
      10. Do not second-guess unless you have good reason to believe the second answer is definitely more correct
      11. Cross out original answer if you decide another answer is more accurate; do not erase until you are ready to hand your paper in
      12. Answer all questions; guess unless instructed otherwise
      13. Leave time for review

   b. Essay questions
      1. Read each question carefully
      2. Determine exactly what is wanted. Underline key words or phrases.
      3. Decide on outline or paragraph answer
      4. Include many different points and elements unless asked to develop any one or two points or elements
      5. Show impartiality by giving pros and cons unless directed to select one side only
      6. Make and write down any assumptions you find necessary to answer the questions
      7. Watch your English, grammar, punctuation and choice of words
      8. Time your answers; don't crowd material

8) Answering the essay question

Most essay questions can be answered by framing the specific response around several key words or ideas. Here are a few such key words or ideas:

M's: manpower, materials, methods, money, management
P's: purpose, program, policy, plan, procedure, practice, problems, pitfalls, personnel, public relations

    a. Six basic steps in handling problems:
1. Preliminary plan and background development
2. Collect information, data and facts
3. Analyze and interpret information, data and facts
4. Analyze and develop solutions as well as make recommendations
5. Prepare report and sell recommendations
6. Install recommendations and follow up effectiveness

    b. Pitfalls to avoid
1. *Taking things for granted* – A statement of the situation does not necessarily imply that each of the elements is necessarily true; for example, a complaint may be invalid and biased so that all that can be taken for granted is that a complaint has been registered
2. *Considering only one side of a situation* – Wherever possible, indicate several alternatives and then point out the reasons you selected the best one
3. *Failing to indicate follow up* – Whenever your answer indicates action on your part, make certain that you will take proper follow-up action to see how successful your recommendations, procedures or actions turn out to be
4. *Taking too long in answering any single question* – Remember to time your answers properly

IX. AFTER THE TEST

Scoring procedures differ in detail among civil service jurisdictions although the general principles are the same. Whether the papers are hand-scored or graded by machine we have described, they are nearly always graded by number. That is, the person who marks the paper knows only the number – never the name – of the applicant. Not until all the papers have been graded will they be matched with names. If other tests, such as training and experience or oral interview ratings have been given, scores will be combined. Different parts of the examination usually have different weights. For example, the written test might count 60 percent of the final grade, and a rating of training and experience 40 percent. In many jurisdictions, veterans will have a certain number of points added to their grades.

After the final grade has been determined, the names are placed in grade order and an eligible list is established. There are various methods for resolving ties between those who get the same final grade – probably the most common is to place first the name of the person whose application was received first. Job offers are made from the eligible list in the order the names appear on it. You will be notified of your grade and your rank as soon as all these computations have been made. This will be done as rapidly as possible.

People who are found to meet the requirements in the announcement are called "eligibles." Their names are put on a list of eligible candidates. An eligible's chances of getting a job depend on how high he stands on this list and how fast agencies are filling jobs from the list.

When a job is to be filled from a list of eligibles, the agency asks for the names of people on the list of eligibles for that job. When the civil service commission receives this request, it sends to the agency the names of the three people highest on this list. Or, if the job to be filled has specialized requirements, the office sends the agency the names of the top three persons who meet these requirements from the general list.

The appointing officer makes a choice from among the three people whose names were sent to him. If the selected person accepts the appointment, the names of the others are put back on the list to be considered for future openings.

That is the rule in hiring from all kinds of eligible lists, whether they are for typist, carpenter, chemist, or something else. For every vacancy, the appointing officer has his choice of any one of the top three eligibles on the list. This explains why the person whose name is on top of the list sometimes does not get an appointment when some of the persons lower on the list do. If the appointing officer chooses the second or third eligible, the No. 1 eligible does not get a job at once, but stays on the list until he is appointed or the list is terminated.

X. HOW TO PASS THE INTERVIEW TEST

The examination for which you applied requires an oral interview test. You have already taken the written test and you are now being called for the interview test – the final part of the formal examination.

You may think that it is not possible to prepare for an interview test and that there are no procedures to follow during an interview. Our purpose is to point out some things you can do in advance that will help you and some good rules to follow and pitfalls to avoid while you are being interviewed.

What is an interview supposed to test?

The written examination is designed to test the technical knowledge and competence of the candidate; the oral is designed to evaluate intangible qualities, not readily measured otherwise, and to establish a list showing the relative fitness of each candidate – as measured against his competitors – for the position sought. Scoring is not on the basis of "right" and "wrong," but on a sliding scale of values ranging from "not passable" to "outstanding." As a matter of fact, it is possible to achieve a relatively low score without a single "incorrect" answer because of evident weakness in the qualities being measured.

Occasionally, an examination may consist entirely of an oral test – either an individual or a group oral. In such cases, information is sought concerning the technical knowledges and abilities of the candidate, since there has been no written examination for this purpose. More commonly, however, an oral test is used to supplement a written examination.

Who conducts interviews?

The composition of oral boards varies among different jurisdictions. In nearly all, a representative of the personnel department serves as chairman. One of the members of the board may be a representative of the department in which the candidate would work. In some cases, "outside experts" are used, and, frequently, a businessman or some other representative of the general public is asked to serve. Labor and management or other special groups may be represented. The aim is to secure the services of experts in the appropriate field.

However the board is composed, it is a good idea (and not at all improper or unethical) to ascertain in advance of the interview who the members are and what groups they represent. When you are introduced to them, you will have some idea of their backgrounds and interests, and at least you will not stutter and stammer over their names.

What should be done before the interview?

While knowledge about the board members is useful and takes some of the surprise element out of the interview, there is other preparation which is more substantive. It *is* possible to prepare for an oral interview – in several ways:

1) Keep a copy of your application and review it carefully before the interview

This may be the only document before the oral board, and the starting point of the interview. Know what education and experience you have listed there, and the sequence and dates of all of it. Sometimes the board will ask you to review the highlights of your experience for them; you should not have to hem and haw doing it.

2) Study the class specification and the examination announcement

Usually, the oral board has one or both of these to guide them. The qualities, characteristics or knowledges required by the position sought are stated in these documents. They offer valuable clues as to the nature of the oral interview. For example, if the job involves supervisory responsibilities, the announcement will usually indicate that knowledge of modern supervisory methods and the qualifications of the candidate as a supervisor will be tested. If so, you can expect such questions, frequently in the form of a hypothetical situation which you are expected to solve. NEVER go into an oral without knowledge of the duties and responsibilities of the job you seek.

3) Think through each qualification required

Try to visualize the kind of questions you would ask if you were a board member. How well could you answer them? Try especially to appraise your own knowledge and background in each area, *measured against the job sought*, and identify any areas in which you are weak. Be critical and realistic – do not flatter yourself.

4) Do some general reading in areas in which you feel you may be weak

For example, if the job involves supervision and your past experience has NOT, some general reading in supervisory methods and practices, particularly in the field of human relations, might be useful. Do NOT study agency procedures or detailed manuals. The oral board will be testing your understanding and capacity, not your memory.

5) Get a good night's sleep and watch your general health and mental attitude

You will want a clear head at the interview. Take care of a cold or any other minor ailment, and of course, no hangovers.

What should be done on the day of the interview?

Now comes the day of the interview itself. Give yourself plenty of time to get there. Plan to arrive somewhat ahead of the scheduled time, particularly if your appointment is in the fore part of the day. If a previous candidate fails to appear, the board might be ready for you a bit early. By early afternoon an oral board is almost invariably behind schedule if there are many candidates, and you may have to wait.

Take along a book or magazine to read, or your application to review, but leave any extraneous material in the waiting room when you go in for your interview. In any event, relax and compose yourself.

The matter of dress is important. The board is forming impressions about you – from your experience, your manners, your attitude, and your appearance. Give your personal appearance careful attention. Dress your best, but not your flashiest. Choose conservative, appropriate clothing, and be sure it is immaculate. This is a business interview, and your appearance should indicate that you regard it as such. Besides, being well groomed and properly dressed will help boost your confidence.

Sooner or later, someone will call your name and escort you into the interview room. *This is it.* From here on you are on your own. It is too late for any more preparation. But remember, you asked for this opportunity to prove your fitness, and you are here because your request was granted.

What happens when you go in?

The usual sequence of events will be as follows: The clerk (who is often the board stenographer) will introduce you to the chairman of the oral board, who will introduce you to the other members of the board. Acknowledge the introductions before you sit down. Do not be surprised if you find a microphone facing you or a stenotypist sitting by. Oral interviews are usually recorded in the event of an appeal or other review.

Usually the chairman of the board will open the interview by reviewing the highlights of your education and work experience from your application – primarily for the benefit of the other members of the board, as well as to get the material into the record. Do not interrupt or comment unless there is an error or significant misinterpretation; if that is the case, do not hesitate. But do not quibble about insignificant matters. Also, he will usually ask you some question about your education, experience or your present job – partly to get you to start talking and to establish the interviewing "rapport." He may start the actual questioning, or turn it over to one of the other members. Frequently, each member undertakes the questioning on a particular area, one in which he is perhaps most competent, so you can expect each member to participate in the examination. Because time is limited, you may also expect some rather abrupt switches in the direction the questioning takes, so do not be upset by it. Normally, a board member will not pursue a single line of questioning unless he discovers a particular strength or weakness.

After each member has participated, the chairman will usually ask whether any member has any further questions, then will ask you if you have anything you wish to add. Unless you are expecting this question, it may floor you. Worse, it may start you off on an extended, extemporaneous speech. The board is not usually seeking more information. The question is principally to offer you a last opportunity to present further qualifications or to indicate that you have nothing to add. So, if you feel that a significant qualification or characteristic has been overlooked, it is proper to point it out in a sentence or so. Do not compliment the board on the thoroughness of their examination – they have been sketchy, and you know it. If you wish, merely say, "No thank you, I have nothing further to add." This is a point where you can "talk yourself out" of a good impression or fail to present an important bit of information. Remember, *you close the interview yourself.*

The chairman will then say, "That is all, Mr. _____, thank you." Do not be startled; the interview is over, and quicker than you think. Thank him, gather your belongings and take your leave. Save your sigh of relief for the other side of the door.

How to put your best foot forward

Throughout this entire process, you may feel that the board individually and collectively is trying to pierce your defenses, seek out your hidden weaknesses and embarrass and confuse you. Actually, this is not true. They are obliged to make an appraisal of your qualifications for the job you are seeking, and they want to see you in your best light. Remember, they must interview all candidates and a non-cooperative candidate may become a failure in spite of their best efforts to bring out his qualifications. Here are 15 suggestions that will help you:

1) Be natural – Keep your attitude confident, not cocky

If you are not confident that you can do the job, do not expect the board to be. Do not apologize for your weaknesses, try to bring out your strong points. The board is interested in a positive, not negative, presentation. Cockiness will antagonize any board member and make him wonder if you are covering up a weakness by a false show of strength.

2) Get comfortable, but don't lounge or sprawl

Sit erectly but not stiffly. A careless posture may lead the board to conclude that you are careless in other things, or at least that you are not impressed by the importance of the occasion. Either conclusion is natural, even if incorrect. Do not fuss with your clothing, a pencil or an ashtray. Your hands may occasionally be useful to emphasize a point; do not let them become a point of distraction.

3) Do not wisecrack or make small talk

This is a serious situation, and your attitude should show that you consider it as such. Further, the time of the board is limited – they do not want to waste it, and neither should you.

4) Do not exaggerate your experience or abilities

In the first place, from information in the application or other interviews and sources, the board may know more about you than you think. Secondly, you probably will not get away with it. An experienced board is rather adept at spotting such a situation, so do not take the chance.

5) If you know a board member, do not make a point of it, yet do not hide it

Certainly you are not fooling him, and probably not the other members of the board. Do not try to take advantage of your acquaintanceship – it will probably do you little good.

6) Do not dominate the interview

Let the board do that. They will give you the clues – do not assume that you have to do all the talking. Realize that the board has a number of questions to ask you, and do not try to take up all the interview time by showing off your extensive knowledge of the answer to the first one.

7) Be attentive

You only have 20 minutes or so, and you should keep your attention at its sharpest throughout. When a member is addressing a problem or question to you, give him your undivided attention. Address your reply principally to him, but do not exclude the other board members.

8) Do not interrupt

A board member may be stating a problem for you to analyze. He will ask you a question when the time comes. Let him state the problem, and wait for the question.

9) Make sure you understand the question

Do not try to answer until you are sure what the question is. If it is not clear, restate it in your own words or ask the board member to clarify it for you. However, do not haggle about minor elements.

10) Reply promptly but not hastily

A common entry on oral board rating sheets is "candidate responded readily," or "candidate hesitated in replies." Respond as promptly and quickly as you can, but do not jump to a hasty, ill-considered answer.

11) Do not be peremptory in your answers

A brief answer is proper – but do not fire your answer back. That is a losing game from your point of view. The board member can probably ask questions much faster than you can answer them.

12) Do not try to create the answer you think the board member wants

He is interested in what kind of mind you have and how it works – not in playing games. Furthermore, he can usually spot this practice and will actually grade you down on it.

13) Do not switch sides in your reply merely to agree with a board member

Frequently, a member will take a contrary position merely to draw you out and to see if you are willing and able to defend your point of view. Do not start a debate, yet do not surrender a good position. If a position is worth taking, it is worth defending.

14) Do not be afraid to admit an error in judgment if you are shown to be wrong

The board knows that you are forced to reply without any opportunity for careful consideration. Your answer may be demonstrably wrong. If so, admit it and get on with the interview.

15) Do not dwell at length on your present job

The opening question may relate to your present assignment. Answer the question but do not go into an extended discussion. You are being examined for a *new* job, not your present one. As a matter of fact, try to phrase ALL your answers in terms of the job for which you are being examined.

Basis of Rating

Probably you will forget most of these "do's" and "don'ts" when you walk into the oral interview room. Even remembering them all will not ensure you a passing grade. Perhaps you did not have the qualifications in the first place. But remembering them will help you to put your best foot forward, without treading on the toes of the board members.

Rumor and popular opinion to the contrary notwithstanding, an oral board wants you to make the best appearance possible. They know you are under pressure – but they also want to see how you respond to it as a guide to what your reaction would be under the pressures of the job you seek. They will be influenced by the degree of poise you display, the personal traits you show and the manner in which you respond.

EXAMINATION SECTION

EXAMINATION SECTION
TEST 1

DIRECTIONS: Each question or incomplete statement is followed by several suggested answers or completions. Select the one that BEST answers the question or completes the statement. *PRINT THE LETTER OF THE CORRECT ANSWER IN THE SPACE AT THE RIGHT.*

1. Of the following, the one which is NOT considered to be a duty of the assistant is to
   A. interview the patients
   B. administer local anaesthesia to a patient
   C. take the temperature of patients
   D. aid the patient in preparing for a medical examination

1.___

2. Assume that a patient appears at your clinic at 11:00 on a busy day while you are on duty in the reception room. He says that he missed his 9:00 appointment and that he must return to work within an hour.
The one of the following which is the MOST acceptable course of action for you to take FIRST is to
   A. ask the others who are waiting if they will allow this patient to precede them
   B. immediately schedule another appointment for the patient for the same day in the following week
   C. take the patient to the examining room to see the doctor immediately
   D. explain to the patient that others are waiting and ask him to wait his turn

2.___

3. As an assistant, you will be required to follow certain instructions of the doctor or nurse in the administration of the clinic. Suppose that you have been given some instructions by the doctor which you do not completely understand.
The one of the following which is the MOST advisable course of conduct for you to follow is to
   A. carry out the instructions to the best of your ability
   B. ask another employee in the clinic to interpret the order to you
   C. ask the doctor to repeat the instructions or to clarify them
   D. disregard the instructions and wait until the doctor speaks to you again

3.___

4. As the assistant assigned to a district health center, you are required to interview new patients briefly to determine which clinics they are to go to. There are a number of patients waiting to talk to you. The person whom you are interviewing is Italian and speaks English so poorly that it is almost impossible for you to understand her. She is also very upset and excited. You know that one of the clerks in the eye clinic speaks Italian.

4.___

For you to call that clerk and ask him to act as interpreter is
   A. *inadvisable*; the information you must get is confidential and should not be known to the clerk
   B. *advisable*; the person you are interviewing will be more comfortable in her own language and the interview will, therefore, be completed more quickly
   C. *inadvisable*; the clerk you wish to call may not want to act as interpreter
   D. *advisable*; you will not be responsible for any misunderstanding in this situation if someone else did the interviewing

5. You are assigned to a chest clinic. One Saturday morning, you are alone in the clinic. The doctor has telephoned that he will be delayed and the nurse has not yet reported. One of the regular clinic patients begins coughing while she is talking to you and has a severe hemorrhage.
   The BEST procedure for you to follow in this situation is to
   A. give the patient a stimulant and apply a cold compress to the back of the neck
   B. look in the other clinics to see if there is anyone else on duty
   C. do nothing until the doctor comes in
   D. call the police for an ambulance

   5.___

6. Suppose that you are assigned to interviewing incoming patients for certain routine information in a busy dental clinic. You learn that some patients go to the eye clinic after you have interviewed them where another assistant interviews them for the same information. The two sets of information are to be kept in permanent card files, in two separate clinic offices.
   Of the following suggestions which you might make to your supervisor, the one which would prove to be MOST helpful in simplifying this procedure would be for you to
   A. continue to record the information separately so that you can check your records with those of the other assistant for possible errors
   B. send the patient to the other clinic first since they may need more information than you do
   C. fill out two record cards and forward one card to the other clinic
   D. send your record card to the other clinic with the patient after he has been examined by the doctor

   6.___

7. Suppose that a visitor calls at your clinic and requests information concerning the medical history of a patient.
   Of the following, the MOST acceptable action for you to take is to
   A. ask him why he wants the information so that you may determine if there is sufficient reason for you to give him the information

   7.___

B. give him the information readily as this will foster favorable public relations

C. refer him to the doctor who examined the patient as he is in a better position to know the patient's medical history

D. explain that you cannot give out such information as it is strictly confidential and suggest that he write to the department for the information

8. To equip a corner of the outer office of a health center with toys is

    8.___

A. *advisable*; the children will be occupied while waiting and, therefore, will be more manageable during the doctor's examination and treatment

B. *inadvisable*; the child may become too absorbed in play to submit to examination

C. *advisable*; the children will be so absorbed in play that they will not be aware of whatever discomfort is caused by treatment

D. *inadvisable*; playing may overstimulate the child and thus cause inaccurate results in the examination

9. While working in a clinic, you discover some obvious inconsistencies in the filing system as a whole. You also have in mind a corrective measure which you would like to see put into practice.

    9.___

The one of the following which is the MOST acceptable procedure for you to follow is to

A. try out your new system for a few days to determine its success before discussing it with your supervisor

B. explain the probable advantages of your proposed plan to your supervisor and secure his approval before making any changes

C. continue working under the old procedure until the inconsistencies become apparent to the rest of the staff

D. collect sufficient evidence to prove the obvious inconsistencies in the present filing system in order to convince your supervisor that the system is unsatisfactory

10. Assume that you are in charge of the patients' files in the health center to which you are assigned. The record cards of the individual patients are filed alphabetically according to the name of the patient. You want to make it easier to pick out the cards of those patients who are under treatment for any one of five indicated diseases. Of the following, the procedure which would be MOST helpful for this purpose would be to

    10.___

A. insert the card of each patient having one of the five diseases into a special folder

B. use a different size card for each of the five diseases

  C. use a different color card for each of the five
    diseases
  D. underline the name of the disease on each card in
    the file

11. Assume that you are assigned to the chest clinic where 11.___
  you are responsible for the patients' x-ray records.
  The doctor in charge tells you that in an old group of
  about 250 disarranged pictures, he thinks there may be
  several instances in which more than one record exists
  for the same patient. He asks you to pick out any such
  records and give them to him.
  Of the following, the BEST procedure for you to follow
  FIRST is to
    A. look at each record in turn, number it, and make a
      list of the numbers and corresponding names
    B. go through the records quickly and pick out those
      names which you remember
    C. arrange the records in alphabetical order according
      to the names of the patients
    D. list the names of all the patients whose records
      appear in the group

12. As an assistant, one of your principal duties is the 12.___
  proper maintenance of the supply cabinet of the clinic
  to which you are assigned. Upon inspecting the cabinet,
  you find several large containers with identical labels.
  However, these contain pills of different color and shapes.
  Of the following, the MOST acceptable course of conduct
  for you to follow is to
    A. attempt to sort the pills and relabel them on the
      basis of your own knowledge
    B. throw all of the pills away to make certain they will
      not be misused
    C. inform the doctor that you have relabeled the con-
      tainers after sorting the pills
    D. inform the doctor of the situation so that he may
      decide what is to be done

13. Assume that a patient arrives at the clinic and demands 13.___
  an immediate appointment at a time when the doctor is
  busy.
  Of the following, the action which is MOST acceptable
  for you to take is to
    A. give the patient a sedative to quiet his nerves and
      guide him to an unoccupied examination room to rest
    B. explain to the patient that the doctor is busy and
      ask him to be seated in the waiting room
    C. ask the doctor to examine the patient immediately
    D. talk to the patient until the doctor is ready

14. One of your duties in the clinic is the weighing and   14.___
    measurement of adult patients.
    Of the following, the procedure which is NOT necessary
    to secure accurate weighing of patients is
        A. daily testing and adjustment of the scale for
           accurate balance
        B. instructing the patient to stand firmly in the
           center of the scale
        C. noting what type of clothing the patient is wearing
        D. placing a clean paper towel on the scale before
           each patient is weighed

15. Suppose that a patient in the clinic is in immediate need   15.___
    of first aid for shock.
    The MOST important thing to do first when both the doctor
    and nurse are absent is to
        A. make the patient as comfortable as possible and
           administer a sedative
        B. keep the patient on his feet and moving about in
           order to activate blood circulation throughout the
           body
        C. keep the patient as warm as possible
        D. try to locate the doctor before attempting any
           independent action

16. A patient reports for her scheduled appointment in the   16.___
    pre-natal clinic and tells you, while she is waiting to
    be examined, that she has a very severe pain in her back.
    Of the following, the MOST acceptable action for you to
    take is to
        A. express sympathy and tell her that you yourself once
           had a severe backache for which it was difficult to
           get any relief
        B. tell her politely not to take up your time with her
           ailments as you have other things to do
        C. recommend a liniment which you have used and found
           to be very helpful in such cases
        D. suggest that she speak to the doctor about it when
           he examines her

17. A *tickler system* in a health center may be used as a   17.___
        A. follow-up procedure for the recall of patients
        B. method of charting blood pressure recordings at
           each visit
        C. standard procedure for recording information to be
           included in memoranda to the doctors
        D. series of tests of nervous reactions

18. When papers are filed according to the date of their   18.___
    receipt, they are said to be filed
        A. numerically   B. geographically
        C. chronologically   D. alphabetically

19. The one of the following which is the MOST important   19.___
    requirement of a good filing system is that
    A. the expense of installation and operation be low
    B. papers be found easily when needed
    C. the system be capable of any amount of expansion
       which may be necessary in the future
    D. the filing system have a cross-reference index

Questions 20-24.

DIRECTIONS: Questions 20 through 24 consist of a group of names
             which are to be arranged in alphabetical order for
             filing.

20. Of the following, the name which should be filed FIRST is   20.___
    A. Joseph J. Meadeen   B. Gerard L. Meader
    C. John F. Madcar   D. Philip F. Malder

21. Of the following, the name which should be filed LAST is   21.___
    A. Stephen Fischer   B. Benjamin Fitchmann
    C. Thomas Fishman   D. Augustus S. Fisher

22. The name which should be filed SECOND is   22.___
    A. Yeatman, Frances   B. Yeaton, C.S.
    C. Yeatman, R.M.   D. Yeats, John

23. The name which should be filed THIRD is   23.___
    A. Hauser, Ann   B. Hauptmann, Jane
    C. Hauster, Mary   D. Hauprich, Julia

24. The name which should be filed SECOND is   24.___
    A. Flora McDougall   B. Fred E. MacDowell
    C. Juanita Mendez   D. James A. Madden

25. The *initial* contact is of great importance in setting a   25.___
    pattern for future relations.
    The word *initial*, as used in this sentence, means MOST
    NEARLY
       A. first   B. written   C. direct   D. hidden

26. The doctor prescribed a diet which was *adequate* for the   26.___
    patient's needs.
    The word *adequate*, as used in this sentence, means MOST
    NEARLY
       A. insufficient   B. unusual
       C. required   D. enough

27. The child was reported to be suffering from a vitamin   27.___
    deficiency.
    The word *deficiency*, as used in this sentence, means MOST
    NEARLY
       A. surplus   B. infection   C. shortage   D. injury

28. In obtaining medical case data, a medical record libra-   28.___
    rian should discourage the patient from giving *irrelevant*
    information.
    The word *irrelevant*, as used in this sentence means MOST
    NEARLY
        A. too detailed   B. pertaining to relatives
        C. insufficient   D. inappropriate

29. The doctor requested that a *tentative* appointment be   29.___
    made for the patient.
    The word *tentative*, as used in this sentence, means MOST
    NEARLY
        A. definite   B. subject to change
        C. later   D. of short duration

30. The black plague resulted in an usually high *mortality*   30.___
    rate in the population of Europe.
    The term *mortality rate*, as used in this sentence, means
    MOST NEARLY
        A. future immunity of the people
        B. death rate
        C. general weakening of the health of the people
        D. sickness rate

31. The public health assistant was asked to file a number   31.___
    of *identical* reports on the case.
    The word *identical*, as used in this sentence, means MOST
    NEARLY
        A. accurate   B. detailed   C. same   D. different

32. The nurse assisted in the *biopsy* of the patient.   32.___
    The word *biopsy*, as used in this sentence, means MOST
    NEARLY
        A. autopsy
        B. excision and diagnostic study of tissue
        C. biography and health history
        D. administering of anesthesia

33. The assistant noted that the swelling on the patient's   33.___
    face had *subsided*.
    The word *subsided*, as used in this sentence, means MOST
    NEARLY
        A. become aggravated   B. increased
        C. vanished   D. abated

34. The patient was given food *intravenously*.   34.___
    The word *intravenously*, as used in this sentence, means
    MOST NEARLY
        A. orally   B. against his will
        C. through the veins   D. without condiment

Questions 35-40.

DIRECTIONS: Questions 35 through 40 are to be answered on the
basis of the chart below.

SEMI-ANNUAL REPORT OF EXPENDITURES FOR SUPPLIES AND EQUIPMENT

Health Center X - January to June

| MONTH | CLINIC | | | | | |
	BABY	CHEST	DENTAL	PRE-NATAL	X-RAY	TOTAL
January	$ 456.32	$ 204.28	$ 723.22	$ 436.29	$ 153.25	$ 1,973.3
February	425.59	225.27	743.33	452.51	174.42	2,021.1
March	631.93	226.35	716.29	429.33	173.37	2,177.2
April	587.27	321.42	729.37	397.27	185.28	2,220.6
May	535.22	275.52	750.54	335.23	184.97	2,081.4
June	539.20	226.80	755.67	394.25	181.08	2,097.0
Total	$3,175.53	$1,479.64	$4,418.42	$2,444.88	$1,052.37	$12,570.8

35.   On the basis of the above chart, the TOTAL expenses of
the dental clinic exceed the total expenses of the baby
clinic for the six-month period by
A. $1,242.89   B. $1,243.79   C. $1,342.79   D. $1,343.89

35.____

36.   The total expenses for the month of January for Health
Center X EXCEED the total expenses of the chest clinic
for the six-month period by
A. $473.82   B. $483.72   C. $484.72   D. $493.72

36.____

37.   The expenditures for the entire Health Center were
HIGHEST during the month of
A. February   B. March   C. April   D. June

37.____

38.   If the total number of patients treated at the Health
Center during February was 632, the APPROXIMATE cost per
patient for the month of February is
A. $3.20   B. $12.50   C. $21.00   D. $31.90

38.____

39.   The TOTAL expenditure for the dental clinic for the six-
month period is
A. *more* than double the total expenses of the Health
Center for March
B. *less* than one-fourth the total expenses of the Health
Center for the six-month period
C. *more* than double the total expenses of the Health
Center for April
D. *less* than the combined totals for the six-month
period of expenses for the baby and x-ray clinics

39.____

40. The TOTAL expenditure for the first three months for the   40.___
   baby clinic is
   A. *greater* than the total expenses for the baby clinic
      for the last three months
   B. *less* than the total expenses for the chest clinic
      for the entire six-month period
   C. *less* than the total expenses for the baby clinic for
      the last three months
   D. *greater* than the total expenses for the pre-natal
      clinic for the entire six-month period

KEY (CORRECT ANSWERS)

1.	B	11.	C	21.	B	31.	C
2.	A	12.	D	22.	C	32.	B
3.	C	13.	B	23.	A	33.	D
4.	B	14.	D	24.	D	34.	C
5.	D	15.	C	25.	A	35.	A
6.	C	16.	D	26.	D	36.	D
7.	D	17.	A	27.	C	37.	C
8.	A	18.	C	28.	D	38.	A
9.	B	19.	B	29.	B	39.	A
10.	C	20.	C	30.	B	40.	C

TEST 2

DIRECTIONS: Each question or incomplete statement is followed by several suggested answers or completions. Select the one that BEST answers the question or completes the statement. *PRINT THE LETTER OF THE CORRECT ANSWER IN THE SPACE AT THE RIGHT.*

1. For an employee to address callers at the clinic by name is   1.___
   A. *advisable*; this is a courtesy that everyone appreciates
   B. *inadvisable*; it would be very embarrassing if she greeted a patient by the wrong name
   C. *advisable*; this assures the patient that the assistant is concentrating on her work
   D. *inadvisable*; patients will tend to take advantage of this display of familiarity

2. One of your duties is to get certain preliminary informa-   2.___
   tion from a new patient before giving him or her an
   appointment with the doctor for a later day. The data
   are to be entered on a permanent record card. Assume
   that you are interviewing a woman who speaks very broken
   English and asks if she can talk to you in Spanish. You
   speak some Spanish and are able to get most of the
   information from her, but are unable to understand a few
   of her answers.
   The one of the following which is the BEST action for you
   to take is to
   A. tell the woman you can't understand her and ask her to come back with an interpreter
   B. fill in on the card all the necessary data as best you can
   C. fill in the information you are certain to have understood correctly, and, at the time of the next appointment, point out to the doctor the omissions
   D. write out for the woman the questions you have not answered on the card and ask her to bring back the answers in writing, in English, the next time she comes

3. Assume that the doctor who is to take charge of the   3.___
   morning session of your clinic has been unavoidably
   detained and arrives an hour late, at 10 A.M.
   The one of the following which is the BEST action for
   you to take is to
   A. ask the patients who have arrived for the appointment between 9 and 10:00 to come back at another time
   B. ask all patients if they can wait; if not, give them appointments for another time
   C. say nothing to any of the patients
   D. ask the patients who had appointments for the last hour of the session to come back at another time

4. Assume that you are put in charge of a medicine supply   4.___
cabinet and you note two identical bottles, one containing a harmless liquid, the other a poisonous substance.
You should
    A. make certain that both bottles are clearly labeled
       at all times
    B. make certain that the bottle containing the poisonous
       substance is clearly labeled at all times
    C. pour the liquids over into different shaped bottles
    D. keep the bottles on two different shelves

5. Assume that a patient with a painful shoulder comes in   5.___
during the doctor's absence and asks you to give him a
treatment such as the doctor had prescribed for him some
months earlier.
You should
    A. comply with the request since the difficulty is
       obviously a relapse
    B. give the patient a sedative and suggest that he call
       for a future appointment if the pain does not subside
    C. ask him to return later when the doctor will be in
    D. explain that, since you are not a registered nurse,
       you are not qualified to give treatment

6. A patient telephones the clinic before the doctor arrives   6.___
and says that the medicine the doctor prescribed for her
makes her nauseous. She wants to know whether she should
continue taking it.
The one of the following steps which you should take
FIRST is to
    A. advise her to stop taking the medication if it is
       not effective
    B. suggest that she continue taking the medicine for
       another week to see if the nausea stops
    C. say that you will inform the doctor and call her back
    D. recommend that she check the accuracy of the pre-
       scription with the pharmacist

7. Assume that one of the medicines in your supply cabinet   7.___
is one which deteriorates within a certain period of time,
and becomes ineffective after that time. According to
instructions, you reorder the medicine periodically, so
that when the old supply becomes ineffective a fresh
supply is on hand. You find, however, that only a small
quantity from each bottle is being used, and the major
portion has to be thrown away.
The one of the following which is the BEST procedure for
you to follow is to
    A. continue to order as before, since you cannot prevent
       the medicine from spoiling
    B. wait with the fresh order until the old supply has
       been used up
    C. order periodically as before, but in smaller quanti-
       ties
    D. order periodically, but at greater intervals, so
       that more of the medicine will be used up

8. Assume that you are charged with the weekly weighing of a   8.___
    certain group of children attending your clinic. Your
    doctor instructs you to fill out a certain card form
    for any child whose weight differs by 5% or more from
    the previous week's reading. One morning, you weigh five
    of these children. Child A weighs 63 lbs., B, 54 lbs.,
    C, 47½ lbs., D, 57 lbs., and E, 61 lbs. The previous
    week's readings were: A, 65 lbs.; B, 51 lbs.; C, 50 lbs.;
    D, 59½ lbs.; E, 56½ lbs.
    The children for whom you will make out cards will be
    - A. A, B, and C   B. B and E
    - C. A, C, D, and E   D. B, C, and E

9. A mother comes to the health center with an infant who   9.___
    appears to be ill. As she comes in, she tells you she
    believes the child may have caught the measles from a
    neighbor's child who is just recovering from the disease.
    The BEST of the following actions for you to take is to
    - A. tell the mother to take a seat and wait her turn to
      see the doctor
    - B. ask the mother if she wants to take a chance on a
      cancelled appointment, as the doctor's schedule is
      filled for the day
    - C. scold the mother for coming in without an appoint-
      ment and arrange for an appointment on the next
      clinic day
    - D. take the mother and child into a vacant examination
      room and inform the doctor at once

10. Assume that you notice that one of the drugs in your   10.___
     supply cabinet has changed color. It is not on the list
     of drugs which deteriorate and which must be reordered
     periodically.
     The one of the following which is the BEST action for you
     to take is to
     - A. order a new supply of the drug immediately
     - B. report the matter to the doctor immediately
     - C. ignore the change in the drug, as it is not caused
       by deterioration
     - D. point out the change to the doctor the next time he
       asks for the drug

11. To use screw caps on medicine bottles in preference to   11.___
     glass stoppers is
     - A. *wise*; screw caps are more attractive
     - B. *unwise*; glass stoppers are less expensive
     - C. *wise*; screw caps afford more protection to the lip
       of the bottle
     - D. *unwise*; glass stoppers are often interchangeable for
       several bottles

12. The one of the following which is the LEAST important   12.___
    precaution to take in connection with the pouring of a
    dose of medicine from a bottle into a glass is to
    A. wear sterile rubber gloves while pouring
    B. hold the label on the bottle uppermost while pouring
    C. clean the rim of the bottle after pouring
    D. make certain the medicine isn't left around for any
       time in an unmarked glass

13. To cover a typed label on a medicine bottle with shellac   13.___
    is
    A. *inadvisable*; the shellac may have a chemical reaction
       on the drug
    B. *advisable*; the label will become waterproof and the
       printing on it remain legible
    C. *inadvisable*; the shellac will cause the printing on
       the label to become illegible
    D. *advisable*; the shellac will prevent the bottle from
       breaking in case it is dropped

14. The one of the following which is the MOST valid reason   14.___
    for a patient's needing a prescription in order to obtain
    a certain drug is that the drug is
    A. poisonous   B. habit-forming
    C. expensive   D. potent

15. While a growing health consciousness is apparent here   15.___
    and in many other countries, our knowledge of how to
    prevent and control disease far exceeds its application.
    This statement means MOST NEARLY that
    A. much of our knowledge of how to improve public health
       is not put into practice
    B. there has been little increase in our knowledge of
       disease prevention and control
    C. some of our knowledge on control of diseases is
       impossible to put into practice
    D. there has been no improvement in the prevention and
       control of disease

16. Developments in the field of nutrition have been an   16.___
    important part of medical progress. Not only have dietary
    cures been discovered for true nutritional diseases but,
    in almost every branch of medicine and surgery, therapy
    has been improved by more scientific methods of feeding.
    The one of the following which is the MOST accurate
    statement on the basis of the above paragraph is that
    A. nutrition plays a minor role in medicine
    B. dietary cures have therapeutic values only in cases
       of nutritional diseases
    C. proper nutrition is important in the cure of diseases
       in almost every branch of medicine
    D. nutritional diseases can be cured only by special
       diets

17. An individual may be wholly immune to one disease and
    ultra-susceptible to another; and such immunity, which
    may be born with the individual or acquired, has absolute-
    ly no relation to physique, robustness, or great vitality.
    The one of the following which is the MOST accurate state-
    ment on the basis of this paragraph is that
    A. an adult who is immune to a disease must have been
       immune to that disease as a child
    B. a person who is susceptible to one disease has a
       tendency to be susceptible to all diseases
    C. a person of poor physique and low vitality may never-
       theless be immune to certain diseases
    D. persons of low vitality are more susceptible to
       diseases than persons of great vitality

17.___

18. If the doctor is in <u>consultation</u> with another doctor, he
    should not be disturbed.
    As used in this sentence, the word *consultation* means
    MOST NEARLY
    A. conference   B. operation
    C. agreement   D. argument

18.___

19. A nurse should not <u>prescribe</u> for patients without the
    doctor's instructions.
    As used in this sentence, the word *prescribe* means MOST
    NEARLY
    A. explain the cuases of illness
    B. ascertain the case history
    C. determine the appointment time
    D. recommend treatment

19.___

20. The doctor has the right to <u>refer</u> patients to the hospital.
    As used in this sentence, the word *refer* means MOST
    NEARLY
    A. accept   B. admit   C. direct   D. accompany

20.___

21. An <u>antidote</u> is an agent which
    A. allays pain
    B. counteracts the effects of a poison
    C. reduces acidity
    D. stimulates the heart

21.___

22. Physical <u>therapy</u> has an important place in medicine.
    As used in this sentence, the word *therapy* means MOST
    NEARLY
    A. massage   B. treatment
    C. exercise   D. examination

22.___

23. Doctors must not advertise or in any way <u>solicit</u> patients.
    As used in this sentence, the word *solicit* means MOST
    NEARLY
    A. actively seek   B. greet
    C. exploit   D. deliberately hurt

23.___

24. After examining the patient, the doctor indicated the   24.___
   <u>prognosis</u> of the illness.
   As used in this sentence, the word *prognosis* means MOST
   NEARLY
       A. probable course   B. cause
       C. treatment   D. past history

25. A doctor practicing *obstetrics* deals with   25.___
       A. glandular disorders   B. deformities of the bones
       C. pregnancy   D. children's diseases

26. The patient's condition was aggravated by a severe case   26.___
   of <u>phobia</u>.
   The word *phobia* means MOST NEARLY
       A. fever   B. apathy
       C. indigestion   D. fear

27. Neglect of immediate treatment may cause an illness to   27.___
   become <u>chronic</u>.
   The word *chronic* means MOST NEARLY
       A. incurable   B. painful
       C. prolonged   D. contagious

28. The one of the following which is NOT generally used to   28.___
   alleviate pain is
       A. aspirin   B. morphine   C. cocaine   D. quinine

29. The administration of a drug subcutaneously means adminis-   29.___
   tration by
       A. mouth
       B. injection beneath the skin
       C. application on the surface of the skin
       D. rectum

30. The one of the following which is NOT a disinfectant is   30.___
       A. boiling water   B. iodine
       C. formaldehyde   D. novocain

31. The one of the following which is LEAST related to the   31.___
   pulse rate of an individual is his
       A. blood pressure   B. temperature
       C. weight   D. emotional state

32. The one of the following which denotes normal vision is   32.___
       A. 20/10   B. 20/20   C. 20/30   D. 20/40

33. Of the following, the temperature which is MOST desirable   33.___
   for a babies' weighing room in a health center is _____°F.
       A. 60-62   B. 65-68   C. 75-77   D. 85-88

34. Of the following, it is MOST advisable for the operator   34.___
   to wear dark glasses during treatments by
       A. x-ray   B. infrared radiation
       C. diathermy   D. ultraviolet radiation

35. Of the following, the BEST method of sterilizing glass-   35.___
    ware for surgical purposes is by means of
    A. immersion in boiling water
    B. steaming under pressure
    C. cold sterilization
    D. washing thoroughly with soap and water

36. The apparatus used for sterilizing medical equipment by   36.___
    means of steam under pressure is the
    A. autoclave   B. manometer   C. catheter   D. reamer

37. After each use of a thermometer, it should be   37.___
    A. held under hot water for several minutes
    B. disinfected in a chemical solution
    C. rinsed in cold water
    D. wiped clean with cotton

38. The LEAST desirable action to take in administering first   38.___
    aid to a person suffering from shock is to
    A. give the patient some aromatic spirits of ammonia
    B. place the patient in a reclining position and
       elevate his legs
    C. loosen any tight clothing and place a pillow under
       his head
    D. place a hot water bottle near the patient's feet

39. Of the following symptoms, the one which does NOT   39.___
    generally accompany a fainting spell is
    A. a flushed face
    B. perspiration of the forehead
    C. shallow breathing
    D. a slow pulse

40. Assume that a six-year-old boy is brought to the clinic,   40.___
    bleeding profusely from a scalp wound. The doctor has
    not as yet arrived.
    Of the following, the MOST effective action for you to
    take is to
    A. wash the wound thoroughly with soap and water to
       prevent infection; apply pressure on the bleeding
       point; then treat for shock
    B. place the boy in a comfortable position; apply tinc-
       ture of iodine to the wound to prevent infection;
       then treat for shock
    C. give the patient a stimulant; then attempt to stop
       the bleeding by applying digital pressure
    D. make the boy comfortable; place a compress over the
       wound and bandage snugly; then threat for shock

41. Of the following, the MOST frequently used method for the   41.___
    diagnosis of pulmonary tuberculosis is the
    A. blood test   B. x-ray
    C. metabolism test   D. urinalysis

42. Of the following conditions, the one which may be infec-   42.___
    tious is
    A. diabetes   B. tuberculosis
    C. appendicitis   D. hypertension

43. Of the following, observation of deviations from normal   43.___
    body weight may aid LEAST in determining the presence of
    A. glandular disturbances   B. malnutrition
    C. organic disturbances   D. mental deficiency

44. Leukemia is a disease of the blood characterized by a   44.___
    A. moderate increase in the red cell count and decrease
       in the white cell count
    B. marked decrease in the red cell count and an increase
       in the white cell count
    C. marked increase in the hemoglobin content
    D. marked decrease in the white cell count

45. The one of the following which is MOST commonly used in   45.___
    the treatment of arthritis is
    A. radium   B. an electrocardiogram
    C. a radiograph   D. diathermy

46. The fluoroscope is used CHIEFLY to   46.___
    A. provide a permanent picture of the condition of
       internal organs at a given time
    B. make a chart of the action of the muscles of the
       heart
    C. observe the internal structure and functioning of the
       organs of the body at a given time
    D. produce heat in the tissues of the body

47. A stethoscope is an instrument used for   47.___
    A. determining the blood pressure
    B. taking the body temperature
    C. chest examination
    D. determining the amount of sugar in the blood

48. The Dick test is used to determine susceptibility to   48.___
    A. measles   B. scarlet fever
    C. diphtheria   D. chickenpox

49. The aorta is a(n)   49.___
    A. bone   B. artery   C. ligament   D. nerve

50. The esophagus is part of the   50.___
    A. alimentary canal   B. abdominal wall
    C. mucous membrane   D. circulatory system

51. Of the following, the one which is NOT a blood vessel is   51.___
    the
    A. vein   B. capillary   C. ganglion   D. artery

52. Vital statistics include data relating to
    A. births, deaths, and marriages
    B. the cost of food, clothing, and shelter
    C. the number of children per family unit
    D. diseases and their comparative mortality rates
52.___

53. In filing letters by subject, you should be MOST concerned with the
    A. name of the sender
    B. main topic of the letter
    C. date of the correspondence
    D. alphabetic cross reference
53.___

54. When arranging the record cards of patients in alphabetical order, the one of the following which should be filed THIRD is
    A. Charles A. Clarke   B. James Clark
    C. Joan Carney   D. Mae Cohen
54.___

55. The one of the following names which should be filed FIRST is
    A. Benjamin Dermody   B. Frank Davidson
    C. Matthew Davids   D. Seymour Diana
55.___

Questions 56-60.

DIRECTIONS: Questions 56 through 60 are to be answered on the basis of the chart below.

ATTENDANCE OF PATIENTS AT Y HEALTH CENTER
FOR WEEK OF APRIL 10

Clinic	Number Summoned for				Number Reported to			
	Baby	Chest	Eye	V.D.	Baby	Chest	Eye	V.D.
Monday	30	42	36	38	29	40	33	35
Tuesday	33	29	34	37	30	29	31	36
Wednesday	38	31	45	42	35	30	40	40
Thursday	41	48	41	32	36	45	39	28
Friday	35	37	39	36	33	35	37	32

56. On the basis of the above chart, it is CORRECT to say that
    A. more patients were summoned to the baby clinic than to the chest clinic during the week
    B. the same number of patients were absent from the eye clinic and the baby clinic during the week
    C. more patients reported to the eye clinic than to the chest clinic during the week
    D. more patients were summoned to the V.D. clinic than to the eye clinic during the week
56.___

57. On the basis of the above chart, the daily average number   57.___
of patients summoned to the eye clinic exceeds the daily
average reporting to the eye clinic by
    A. 3   B. 7   C. 11   D. 15

58. The percentage of all patients summoned to Y Health   58.___
Center on Thursday who failed to report for their
appointments is
    A. *less* than 5%
    B. *more* than 5% but less than 10%
    C. *more* than 10% but less than 15%
    D. *more* than 15%

59. The number of patients summoned for the entire week to   59.___
the eye clinic exceeds the number of patients summoned
to the baby clinic by
    A. 6   B. 9   C. 13   D. 18

60. The total number of patients who reported to Y Health   60.___
Center for the week is
    A. 683   B. 693   C. 724   D. 744

Questions 61-80.

DIRECTIONS: Column I below lists words used in medical practice.
Column II lists phrases which describe the words in
Column I. In the space at the right, place the
letter preceding the phrase in Column II which BEST
describes the word in Column I.

COLUMN I	COLUMN II	
61. Abrasion	A. A disturbance of digestion	61.___
62. Aseptic	B. Destroying the germs of disease	62.___
63. Cardiac	C. A general poisoning of the blood	63.___
64. Catarrh	D. An instrument used for injecting fluids	64.___
65. Contamination	E. A scraping off of the skin	65.___
66. Dermatology	F. Free from disease germs	66.___
67. Disinfectant		67.___
68. Dyspepsia	G. An apparatus for viewing internal organs by means of x-rays	68.___
69. Epidemic		69.___
70. Epidermis	H. An instrument for assisting the eye in observing minute objects	70.___

COLUMN I	COLUMN II	
71. Incubation	I. An inoculable immunizing agent	71.___
72. Microscope	J. The extensive prevalence in a community of a disease	72.___
73. Pediatrics		73.___
74. Plasma	K. Chemical product of an organ	74.___
75. Prenatal	L. Preceding birth	75.___
76. Retina	M. Fever	76.___
77. Syphilis	N. The branch of medical science that relates to the skin and its diseases	77.___
78. Syringe		78.___
79. Toxemia	O. Fluid part of the blood	79.___
80. Vaccine	P. The science of the hygienic care of children	80.___

Q. Infection by contact

R. Relating to the heart

S. Inner structure of the eye

T. Outer portion of the skin

U. Pertaining to the ductless gland

V. An infectious venereal disease

W. Pertaining to the hip

X. The development of an infectious disease from the period of infection to that of the appearance of the first symptoms

Y. Simple inflammation of a mucous membrane

Z. An instrument for measuring blood pressure

KEY (CORRECT ANSWERS)

1. A	21. B	41. B	61. E
2. D	22. B	42. B	62. F
3. B	23. A	43. D	63. R
4. A	24. A	44. B	64. Y
5. C	25. C	45. D	65. Q
6. C	26. D	46. C	66. N
7. C	27. C	47. C	67. B
8. D	28. D	48. B	68. A
9. D	29. B	49. B	69. J
10. B	30. D	50. A	70. T
11. C	31. C	51. C	71. X
12. A	32. B	52. A	72. H
13. B	33. C	53. B	73. P
14. B	34. D	54. A	74. O
15. A	35. B	55. C	75. L
16. C	36. A	56. C	76. S
17. C	37. B	57. A	77. V
18. A	38. C	58. B	78. D
19. D	39. A	59. D	79. C
20. C	40. D	60. B	80. I

EXAMINATION SECTION

DIRECTIONS: Each question or incomplete statement is followed by several suggested answers or completions. Select the one that BEST answers the question or completes the statement. *PRINT THE LETTER OF THE CORRECT ANSWER IN THE SPACE AT THE RIGHT.*

1. Assume that you are assigned to a health center. A middle-aged man walks in and says that he doesn't feel well. He complains of a slight pain in the chest and has difficulty breathing.
Of the following actions, the one you should take is to
   A. isolate him immediately as he may have *Asian flu*
   B. find out what he has eaten as he may have food poisoning
   C. ask him to sit down and see if he can catch his breath
   D. see that he is seated and then call a doctor

1.___

2. A baby who has been brought to the health center for an examination has been crying continuously for 20 minutes. The BEST of the following actions you should take is to
   A. have the baby examined by the first available physician
   B. ask the others who are waiting if they would object to the baby being examined out of turn
   C. call the situation to the attention of the nurse in charge
   D. do nothing as there are probably others who are ill and need to see the doctor

2.___

3. Suppose that a mother comes into the health center, carrying a 3-year-old child who is ill. The mother tells you that the child has a temperature of 102°F, his nose is stuffed, and he is sneezing.
For you to seat the mother and child apart from the others who are waiting for the physician is
   A. *correct*; the other children and adults in the clinic should not be exposed to a disease which may be contagious
   B. *incorrect*; the mother might be offended if she were treated differently than the other patients
   C. *correct*; the nurse is in a good position to diagnose patients when the doctor is not available
   D. *incorrect*; you should wait until the physician makes his diagnosis before isolating the child

3.___

4. In the performance of her work, it is not enough that the employee be alert to the immediate demands of her own job; she must be constantly aware of the basic function of the clinic.
This statement means that a worker should view the ultimate purpose of her job as

4.___

    A. giving effective service to patients
    B. getting the most work done in the shortest time
    C. following to the letter all orders given to her
    D. reporting punctually and working diligently

5. While serving at an eye clinic, you are instructed to   5.___
answer the phone by saying, *Eye Clinic, Miss Jones
speaking.*
Of the following, the BEST reason for this practice is
that
    A. it sets the tone for a brief, concise telephone
       conversation
    B. it is the standard practice recommended by the tele-
       phone company and is familiar to callers
    C. the caller will understand that he cannot ask for
       medical information, since you are not a physician
    D. the caller will know whether he is speaking to the
       person he wants to reach

6. If a telephone call is received for a doctor while he is   6.___
examining a patient, it would be BEST to
    A. tell the caller to telephone again when the doctor
       can receive a call
    B. take the caller's telephone number and have the
       doctor return the call when he is free
    C. ask the nature of the call in order to determine if
       it requires the doctor's immediate attention
    D. refer the call to the nurse in charge as she may
       have the information the caller requires

7. Suppose that a patient who attends the clinic has made   7.___
frequent complaints, usually unjustified.
Of the following, the BEST reason for not ignoring
another complaint from her is that
    A. she is likely to take her complaint to a higher level
    B. even though past complaints have been unjustified,
       this particular one may require attention
    C. a patient is often pacified if you pretend that you
       will look into her complaint
    D. no distinction should be made in your attitude toward
       patients

8. Clinic appointments are less likely to be broken if you   8.___
    A. make appointments on dates which are convenient for
       the patients
    B. stress to each patient that a broken appointment
       inconveniences other patients
    C. threaten not to make any more appointments for
       patients who break appointments without a good reason
    D. arrange the schedule of appointments so that patients
       do not have to wait in the clinic

9. Assume that every day the schedule of the clinic is severely disrupted because several patients without appointments must be treated for emergency conditions. Of the following, the BEST suggestion you could make in order to minimize disruption is that
    A. one morning a week be set aside when all emergency cases will be treated
    B. applicants who claim emergency conditions be screened to see which of them really need emergency treatment
    C. unassigned periods be allowed in the schedule in anticipation of emergency cases
    D. the clinic be kept open each evening until all patients have been treated

    9.___

10. Suppose that a woman who is scheduled to appear at 3:30 P.M. comes into the clinic at 10 A.M. and says she is ill and must see the doctor at once. The clinic is already quite crowded.
    It would be BEST for you to
    A. try to determine if she is really ill, since some patients use the claim as a ruse to get prompt attention
    B. tell her to return at the proper time, since the other patients will become disorderly if others are taken before they are
    C. see if the head nurse will take her out of turn, since she may need prompt care
    D. see if a clinic physician is willing to see her, since public reaction would be hostile if the condition of the woman became worse while waiting

    10.___

11. Some authorities advocate that the mother not stay in the same room when a child of 3 or 4 is being treated by the doctor.
    Of the following, the BEST reason for this is that the
    A. mother might become upset if she watches the treatment
    B. child is less likely to accept the doctor's authority
    C. mother will prolong the examination by questioning the doctor about her child
    D. child will mature more rapidly if he is not always accompanied by his mother

    11.___

12. Assume that a patient tells you that he is not going to follow the treatment recommended by the physician because he doesn't have long to live anyway.
    It would be BEST for you to
    A. report the conversation to the physician
    B. point out to the patient that it is foolish to come for treatment if he will not follow the recommendations given him by the physician
    C. explain to the patient that he will live longer and less painfully if he follows the physician's recommendations
    D. try to get a relative in whom the patient has confidence to persuade him to follow the physician's recommendations

    12.___

13. Suppose that a patient who has just received treatment in the clinic complains loudly that she was kept waiting a long time and then received hasty and inadequate treatment.
It is BEST for you to
   A. explain that treatment is necessarily hasty because the clinic is busy
   B. avoid arguing with her, since ill people are often overwrought
   C. tell her she is not qualified to decide whether treatment is adequate
   D. refer the patient back to the physician for completion of treatment

13.___

14. Assume that a patient who has been coming to the clinic for some time asks you, *Do I have a heart condition?*
You know that his clinic record card bears the notation *heart murmur*.
Under these circumstances, it would be BEST for you to tell him
   A. he has a heart murmur, since he obviously knows this and his card gives you the information
   B. he does not have a heart condition, since the doctor would have informed the patient if he wanted him to know about it
   C. not to worry about it since lots of people have a heart condition
   D. to ask the physician whom he has been seeing in the clinic about this

14.___

15. If a 3-year-old child refuses to stay on a scale long enough to be weighed, the BEST of the following actions for you to take is to
   A. obtain the child's weight by first weighing the mother holding the child in her arms, and then weighing the mother alone
   B. insist that the child be weighed so that the other children in the clinic will cooperate when being weighed
   C. ask one of the special officers to assist her in weighing the child
   D. note on the record that the child refused to be weighed and let the physician determine if it is necessary to weigh the child

15.___

16. You have been asked to hand the sterile instruments to the physician while he is changing a dressing. Suppose that halfway through the procedure, the doctor drops the forceps he is using.
Of the following actions, the one that you should take at this time is to
   A. pick up the forceps with your hand and ask the doctor if he will need it any more
   B. pick up the forceps with your hand and place it with other contaminated instruments

16.___

    C. move the forceps out of the way with your foot
    D. use sterile forceps from the cabinet to pick up the forceps from the floor

17. You have been asked to prepare a list of supplies to be reordered for your clinic.
In order for you to determine how much of any item to reorder, it would be MOST important to know
    A. the average amount of the item used in a given period of time
    B. what the item is used for in the clinic
    C. how much storage space is available for these supplies
    D. the cost of each item

17.___

18. Assume that when you open a cabinet in which disinfectants are kept, you find that one of the bottles has no label. However, there is a label on the shelf near the bottle.
Of the following, the BEST action for you to take is to
    A. paste the label on the bottle since it obviously is the label for that bottle
    B. paste the label on the bottle only if the label has the word *disinfectant* clearly marked on it
    C. place the bottle back in the cabinet and ask the nurse in charge what to do
    D. pour the contents of the bottle into the sink, rinse the bottle, and place it in the proper receptacle

18.___

19. After washing and rinsing rubber hot water bottles, hang them upside down with their mouths open. When they are thoroughly dry, inflate them, place the stoppers into the mouths of the bottles, and leave them hanging. If they are to be stored, leave them inflated and place gauze or crushed paper between them.
On the basis of this paragraph, the one of the following statements that is MOST accurate is that, when storing hot water bottles,
    A. they should be stuffed with paper
    B. a free flow of air must circulate around them
    C. care must be taken to prevent their sides from sticking together
    D. they should be placed upside down with their mouths open

19.___

20. In filing, a cross index should be used for a record which
    A. may be filed in either of two places
    B. has been temporarily removed from the file
    C. concerns a patient who is no longer coming to the clinic
    D. will be used to remind patients of appointments

20.___

21. Assume that the cards of patients are kept in alphabetical order. You are given an alphabetical list of persons who have received injections for *Asian flu* at the clinic, and are asked to see if there is a card in the file for each person on the list.
It would be BEST for you to

21.___

A. determine if the number of cards and the number of names on the list are the same
B. place a check mark next to each name on the list for which there is a corresponding card
C. place a check mark on each card for which there is a corresponding name on the list
D. prepare a second list of all cards in the file and place a check mark next to each name for which there is a corresponding name on the first list

22. Assume that there are several clinics within a health center. Patients' cards are filed according to the clinic which they attend, and within each clinic are filed alphabetically. Every Friday you are responsible for filing the cards of all patients who were in the health center during that week. The cards are in mixed order. Of the following, the FIRST step to take is to
    A. arrange the patients' cards in alphabetical order
    B. separate the cards of those patients who attended more than one clinic from all the others
    C. arrange the patients' cards according to the clinic attended
    D. arrange the patients' cards according to the date the patient attended the clinic

22.___

23. Suppose that, in Clinic A, a medical history card is prepared for each new patient. In this clinic, a blood test is made for each patient as a routine procedure. You have been instructed to make out either a blue card for a negative report, or a white card for a positive report, when the laboratory reports of the blood tests are received.
In order to make sure that all reports on the blood tests have been received, you should compare the number of reports received with the number of _____ cards.
    A. medical history   B. blue
    C. white   D. blue and white

23.___

24. Assume that you are in charge of ordering supplies needed for the clinic. When reordering items, it is BEST to
    A. count supplies at the beginning of each month and reorder an item as soon as there is no more of it in stock
    B. determine beforehand the amount of each item which it is necessary to have on hand and reorder the item when the supply falls to this level
    C. reorder each item in sufficient quantity to last half a year so that there will be no danger of running out of supplies
    D. reorder all items at the beginning of each month so that no item needed will be forgotten

24.___

25. It is usually recommended that, when new supplies of any   25.___
    item are received, they be placed beneath or behind
    supplies of the item already in stock.
    Of the following, the BEST reason for this is that this
    procedure
    A. requires less frequent handling of supplies
    B. makes it easier to tell how much of each item you
       have on hand
    C. allows you to use the storage space most effectively
    D. makes it more likely that the older supplies will
       be used first

26. The abbreviation *EEG* refers to a(n)   26.___
    A. examination of the eyes and ears
    B. inflammatory disease of the urinogenital tract
    C. disease of the esophageal structure
    D. examination of the brain

27. The complete destruction of all forms of living micro-   27.___
    organisms is called
    A. decontamination   B. fumigation
    C. sterilization   D. germination

28. A rectal thermometer differs from other fever thermometers   28.___
    in that it has a
    A. longer stem   B. thinner stem
    C. stubby bulb at one end D. slender bulb at one end

29. The one of the following pieces of equipment which is   29.___
    usually used together with a sphygmometer is a
    A. stethoscope   B. watch
    C. fever thermometer   D. hypodermic syringe

30. A curette is a   30.___
    A. healing drug   B. curved scalpel
    C. long hypodermic needle D. scraping instrument

31. The otoscope is used to examine the patient's   31.___
    A. eyes   B. ears   C. mouth   D. lungs

32. A catheter is used   32.___
    A. to close wounds
    B. for withdrawing fluid from a body cavity
    C. to remove cataracts
    D. as a cathartic

33. Of the following pieces of equipment, the one that is   33.___
    required for making a scratch test is a
    A. needle   B. scalpel
    C. capillary tube   D. tourniquet

34. A hemostat is an instrument which is used to   34.___
    A. hold a sterile needle
    B. clamp off a blood vessel
    C. regulate the temperature of a sterilizer
    D. measure oxygen intake

35. Of the following medical supplies, the one that MUST be   35.___
    stored in a tightly sealed bottle is
    A. sodium fluoride
    B. alum
    C. oil of cloves
    D. aromatic spirits of ammonia

36. A person who has been exposed to an infectious disease   36.___
    is called
    A. a contact   B. an incubator
    C. diseased   D. infected

37. A myocardial infarct would occur in the   37.___
    A. heart   B. kidneys   C. lungs   D. spleen

38. The abbreviations WBC and RBC refer to the results of   38.___
    tests of the
    A. basal metabolism   B. blood
    C. blood pressure   D. bony structure

39. When a person's blood pressure is noted as 120/80, it   39.___
    means that his _____ blood pressure is _____.
    A. pulse; 120   B. pulse; 80
    C. systolic; 120   D. systolic; 80

40. The anatomical structure that contains the tonsils and   40.___
    adenoids is the
    A. pharynx   B. larynx   C. trachea   D. sinuses

41. An abscess can BEST be described as a   41.___
    A. loss of sensation
    B. painful tooth
    C. ruptured membrane
    D. localized formation of pus

42. Nephritis is a disease affecting the   42.___
    A. gall bladder   B. larynx
    C. kidney   D. large intestine

43. Hemoglobin is contained in the   43.___
    A. white blood cells   B. lymph fluids
    C. platelets   D. red blood cells

44. Bile is a body fluid that is MOST directly concerned with   44.___
    A. digestion   B. excretion
    C. reproduction   D. metabolism

45. Of the following bones, the one which is located below   45.___
    the waist is the
        A. sternum   B. clavicle   C. tibia   D. humerus

46. The one of the following which is NOT part of the   46.___
    digestive canal is the
        A. esophagus B. larynx   C. duodenum   D. colon

47. The thyroid and the pituitary are part of the _____   47.___
    system.
        A. digestive   B. endocrine
        C. respiratory   D. excretory

48. The one of the following which would be included in a *GU*   48.___
    examination is the
        A. rectum   B. trachea   C. kidneys   D. pancreas

49. Of the following, the one which would be included in the   49.___
    x-ray examination known as a *GI series* is the
        A. colon   B. skull   C. lungs   D. uterus

50. A person who, while not ill himself, may transmit a   50.___
    disease to another person is known as a(n)
        A. breeder   B. incubator
        C. carrier   D. inhibitor

51. Thorough washing of the hands for two minutes with soap   51.___
    and warm water will leave the hands
        A. sterile   B. aseptic
        C. decontaminated   D. partially disinfected

52. The one of the following which is BEST for preparing the   52.___
    skin for an injection is
        A. green soap and water   B. alcohol
        C. phenol   D. formalin

53. A fever thermometer should be cleansed after use by   53.___
    washing it with
        A. soap and cool water   B. warm water only
        C. soap and hot water   D. running cold tap water

54. The FIRST step in cleaning an instrument which has fresh   54.___
    blood on it is to
        A. wash it in hot soapy water
        B. wash it under cool running water
        C. soak it in a boric acid bath
        D. soak it in 70% alcohol

55. If a contaminated nasal speculum cannot be sterilized   55.___
    immediately after use, then the BEST procedure to follow
    until sterilization is possible is to place it
        A. under a piece of dry gauze
        B. in warm water
        C. in alcohol
        D. in a green soap solution

56. A hypodermic needle should always be checked to see if   56.___
it has a good sharp point
    A. when it is being washed
    B. when it is removed from the sterilizer
    C. just before it is sterilized
    D. immediately before an injection

57. Of the following, the LOWEST temperature at which cotton   57.___
goods will be sterilized if placed in an autoclave for
30 minutes is _____°F.
    A. 130   B. 170   C. 200   D. 250

58. Of the following procedures, the one which is BEST for   58.___
sterilizing an ear speculum which is contaminated with
wax is to
    A. scrub in with cold soapy water, rinse in ether, and
       place in boiling water for 20 minutes
    B. soak it in warm water, scrub in cold soapy water,
       rinse with water, and autoclave at 275°F for 10
       minutes
    C. wash it in alcohol, scrub in hot soapy water, rinse
       with water, and place in boiling water for 20 minutes
    D. wash it in 1% Lysol solution, rinse, and autoclave
       at 275°F for 15 minutes

59. Assume that clean water accidentally spilled on the out-   59.___
side of a package of cloth-wrapped hypodermic syringes
which has been sterilized.
Of the following, the BEST action to take is to
    A. leave the package to dry in a sunny, clean place
    B. sterilize the package again
    C. remove the wet cloth and wrap the package in a dry
       sterile cloth
    D. wipe off the package with a clean dry towel and
       later ask the nurse in charge what to do

60. Hypodermic needles should be sterilized by placing them   60.___
in
    A. boiling water for 5 minutes
    B. an autoclave at 15 lbs. pressure for 15 minutes
    C. oil heated to 220°F for 10 minutes
    D. a 1:40 Lysol solution for 10 minutes

61. A cutting instrument should be sterilized by placing it in   61.___
    A. a chemical germicide
    B. an autoclave at 15 lbs. pressure for 20 minutes
    C. boiling water for 20 minutes
    D. a hot air oven at 320°F for 1 hour

62. A fever thermometer used by a patient who has tuberculosis   62.___
should be washed and then placed in _____ minute(s).
    A. boiling water for 10
    B. a hot air oven for 20
    C. a 1:1000 solution of bichloride of mercury for one
    D. an autoclave at 15 lbs. pressure for 15

63. The MOST reliable method of sterilizing a glass syringe   63.___
    is to place it in _____ minutes.
    A. Zephiran chloride 1:1000 solution for 40
    B. oil heated to 250°F for 12
    C. boiling water for 20
    D. an autoclave at 15 lbs. pressure for 20

64. The insides of sterilizers should be cleaned daily with   64.___
    a mild abrasive PRIMARILY to
    A. remove scale
    B. prevent the growth of bacteria
    C. remove blood and other organic matter
    D. prevent acids from damaging the sterilizer

65. Of the following, the BEST reason for giving a patient a   65.___
    jar in which to bring a urine specimen on his next visit
    to the clinic is that the
    A. patient may not have a jar at home
    B. patient may bring the specimen in a jar which is too
       large
    C. patient may bring the specimen in a jar which has not
       been cleaned properly
    D. jar may be misplaced if it is not a jar in which
       urine specimens are usually collected

66. Simply providing nutritional information and recommended   66.___
    low-cost diets to clinic patients has not resulted in
    improved diets for their children.
    The MOST plausible conclusion to draw from this statement
    is that
    A. nutrition is only one factor in improving health
    B. nutrition is of greater value in improving the health
       of adults than in improving the health of children
    C. the health problems of clinic patients are not caused
       by nutritional defects
    D. clinic patients are not using the nutritional informa-
       tion given them

67. Many people who appear to be robust are highly susceptible   67.___
    to disease, and are outlived by many seemingly frail
    people.
    Of the following, the MOST plausible conclusion which may
    be drawn from this statement is that
    A. physical appearance is not a reliable indicator of
       health
    B. frail people take better care of themselves than do
       robust people
    C. disease tends to strike robust people more frequently
       than frail people
    D. robust people tend to overexert themselves more
       often than frail people do

68. The skill of interviewers, the wording of questions, and   68.___
    the willingness of patients to respond freely to questions
    all affect the results of a survey. Reports of surveys of
    patient attitudes toward the health work of the clinic
    are, therefore, valueless unless we also know how the
    surveys were conducted. A recent report that 85% of
    clinic patients were satisfied with clinic service must
    be treated with caution; it may be that another survey
    would have revealed just the opposite!
    On the basis of this paragraph, it is MOST accurate to
    conclude that
        A. survey reports have little value in determining
           patient attitudes
        B. contrary to a recent report, 85% of clinic patients
           are dissatisfied with clinic service
        C. published results of surveys may be misleading unless
           accompanied by knowledge of the methods used
        D. listening to the unsolicited comments of clinic
           patients is of greater value than questioning them
           directly concerning their attitudes

Questions 69-75.

DIRECTIONS: Questions 69 through 75 are to be answered on the
             basis of the following table.

STATISTICAL REPORT OF CLINICS IN XYZ HEALTH CENTER March				
	APPOINTMENTS		PROCEDURES	
Clinic	No. of Appointments Scheduled	No. of Broken Appointments	No. of Diagnostic Procedures	No. of Surgical Procedures
A	1400	260	1910	140
B	730	160	2000	500
C	1250	250	950	130
D	540	90	400	220
E	890	140	1500	280

69. On the basis of the preceding table, the total number of   69.___
    appointments kept for all clinics in the health center
    in March is
        A. 900   B. 3910   C. 4810   D. 5710

70. The percentage of appointments kept in Clinic C during   70.___
    March is
        A. 5%   B. 20%   C. 75%   D. 80%

71. If Clinic A was open for 20 days during March, the average 71.___
    number of appointments scheduled each day at Clinic A is
        A. 57   B. 70   C. 140   D. 280

72. In comparison to the clinic which performed the fewest   72.___
    diagnostic procedures, the clinic which performed the
    MOST diagnostic procedures did _____ as many.
        A. twice   B. three times
        C. four times   D. five times

73. The average number of diagnostic procedures performed   73.___
    for all clinics during March is
        A. 254   B. 676   C. 1352   D. 6760

74. The percentage of all procedures done at Clinic B during   74.___
    March which were surgical procedures is
        A. 2%   B. 2.5%   C. 20%   D. 25%

75. Clinic E used 10 boxes of gauze for its surgical proce-   75.___
    dures during March.
    If Clinic A used gauze at the same rate for its surgical
    procedures, the number of boxes of gauze Clinic A used
    during March is
        A. 3   B. 5   C. 10   D. 14

Questions 76-84.

DIRECTIONS: Each of Questions 76 through 84 consists of four words.
              Three of these words belong together. One word does
              NOT belong with the other three. For each group of
              words, you are to select the one word which does NOT
              belong with the other three words.

76. A. conclude   B. terminate   C. initiate   D. end   76.___

77. A. deficient   B. inadequate   77.___
    C. excessive   D. insufficient

78. A. rare   B. unique   C. unusual   D. frequent   78.___

79. A. unquestionable   B. uncertain   79.___
    C. doubtful   D. indefinite

80. A. stretch   B. contract   C. extend   D. expand   80.___

81. A. accelerate   B. quicken   81.___
    C. accept   D. hasten

82. A. sever   B. rupture   C. rectify   D. tear   82.___

83. A. innocuous B. injurious   C. dangerous D. harmful   83.___

84. A. adulterate   B. contaminate   84.___
    C. taint   D. disinfect

Questions 85-90.

DIRECTIONS: Questions 85 through 90 are to be answered on the basis of the usual rules for alphabetical filing. For each question, indicate in the space at the right the letter preceding the name which should be filed THIRD in alphabetical order.

85. A. Russell Cohen   B. Henry Cohn   85.____
    C. Wesley Chambers   D. Arthur Connors

86. A. Wanda Jenkins   B. Pauline Jennings   86.____
    C. Leslie Jantzenberg   D. Rudy Jensen

87. A. Arnold Wilson   B. Carlton Willson   87.____
    C. Duncan Williamson   D. Ezra Wilston

88. A. Joseph M. Buchman   B. Gustave Bozzerman   88.____
    C. Constantino Brunelli D. Armando Buccino

89. A. Barbara Waverly   B. Corinne Warterdam   89.____
    C. Dennis Waterman   D. Harold Wartman

90. A. Jose Mejia   B. Bernard Mendelsohn 90.____
    C. Antonio Mejias   D. Richard Mazzitelli

Questions 91-100.

DIRECTIONS: Questions 91 through 100 are to be answered on the basis of the usual rules of filing. Column I lists, next to the numbers 91 to 100, the names of 10 clinic patients. Column II lists, next to the letters A to D, the headings of file drawers into which you are to place the records of these patients. For each question, indicate in the space at the right the letter preceding the heading of the file drawer in which the record should be filed.

	COLUMN I		COLUMN II	
91.	Frank Shea	A.	Sab - Sej	91.____
92.	Rose Seaborn	B.	Sek - Sio	92.____
93.	Samuel Smollin	C.	Sip - Soo	93.____
94.	Thomas Shur	D.	Sop - Syz	94.____
95.	Ben Schaefer			95.____
96.	Shirley Strauss			96.____
97.	Harry Spiro			97.____
98.	Dora Skelly			98.____
99.	Sylvia Smith			99.____
100.	Arnold Selz			100.____

KEY (CORRECT ANSWERS)

1. D	26. D	51. D	76. C
2. C	27. C	52. B	77. C
3. A	28. C	53. A	78. D
4. A	29. A	54. B	79. A
5. D	30. D	55. D	80. B
6. C	31. B	56. C	81. C
7. B	32. B	57. D	82. C
8. A	33. A	58. C	83. A
9. C	34. B	59. B	84. D
10. C	35. D	60. B	85. B
11. B	36. A	61. A	86. B
12. A	37. A	62. C	87. A
13. B	38. B	63. D	88. D
14. D	39. C	64. A	89. C
15. A	40. A	65. C	90. C
16. C	41. D	66. D	91. B
17. A	42. C	67. A	92. A
18. D	43. D	68. C	93. C
19. C	44. A	69. B	94. B
20. A	45. C	70. D	95. A
21. B	46. B	71. B	96. D
22. C	47. B	72. D	97. D
23. A	48. C	73. C	98. C
24. B	49. A	74. C	99. C
25. D	50. C	75. B	100. B

EXAMINATION SECTION
TEST 1

DIRECTIONS: Each question or incomplete statement is followed by several suggested answers or completions. Select the one that BEST answers the question or completes the statement. *PRINT THE LETTER OF THE CORRECT ANSWER IN THE SPACE AT THE RIGHT.*

1. An employee should know not only the details of his own job but the main objective of the organization for which he works.
The MAIN objective of a health center may BEST be described as the
   A. orderly and efficient management of the health center
   B. improvement of the health of the community it serves
   C. courteous treatment of patients who are poor
   D. enforcement of the health laws of the city

1.___

2. The MOST appropriate of the following statements for Miss Smith, who works in the cardiac clinic, to make when answering the clinic telephone is:
   A. This is the Cardiac Clinic. Who's calling please?
   B. Hello. This is Miss Smith.
   C. Cardiac Clinic, Miss Smith speaking. May I help you?
   D. Miss Smith speaking. To whom do you wish to speak?

2.___

3. Of the following, the CHIEF reason why you should be familiar with medical terminology is so that you can
   A. be of greatest assistance to the doctors and nurses
   B. answer the patient's questions about their symptoms and treatments
   C. know what supplies to order for the clinic
   D. understand the medical publications which are sent to the clinic

3.___

4. Assume that instructions have been issued in your clinic that medical information is not to be given to patients.
Of the following, the BEST reason for this policy is that
   A. the relationship between the clinic staff and clinic patients, although friendly, should remain impersonal
   B. the health of a patient is a private matter which should not be discussed in public
   C. incorrect medical information might be given to the patient
   D. only the nurse in charge should be permitted to give medical information to patients

4.___

5. Of the following, the BEST reason for keeping clinic records confidential is to
   A. protect the patient who may not want others to know certain information
   B. protect the health station in case errors have been made

5.___

C. prevent publicity about the health station which may keep patients from coming to the clinics
D. avoid the extra work involved in giving out information

6. To give each patient who is to return to the clinic a card   6.___
   with the date of his next appointment written on it is
   A. unnecessary; it is sufficient to tell him when to come back
   B. of little value; some of the patients may not be able to read English
   C. impractical; too much time would be taken up in writing the cards
   D. good practice; the patient would be less likely to forget his next date

7. When setting up a *tickler* file for patients' appointments   7.___
   in your clinic, you should arrange the cards according to the
   A. name of the patient
   B. date when the patient is due in the clinic
   C. condition for which the patient is being treated
   D. name of the doctor

8. Assume that you are responsible for maintaining the   8.___
   patients' record file in the clinic to which you are
   assigned. Frequently, the other clinics in the health
   center where you work borrow record cards from your
   clinic files.
   The BEST way for you to avoid difficulty in locating cards
   which may have been borrowed by other clinics is to
   A. make out a duplicate card for any clinic that wishes to borrow a card from your file
   B. refuse to lend your card to any other clinic unless the other clinic's personnel officer promises to return the card in person
   C. report it to your supervisor if anyone fails to return a card after a reasonable time
   D. have the person who borrows a card fill out an out-of-file card and place it in the file whenever a record card is removed

9. Suppose that you are given an unalphabetized list of 500   9.___
   clinic patients and a set of unalphabetized record cards.
   Your supervisor asks you to determine if there is a record
   card for each patient whose name is on the list.
   For you to first arrange the record cards in alphabetical
   order before checking them with the names on the list is
   A. *desirable*; this will make it easier to check each name on the list against the patients' record cards
   B. *undesirable*; it is just as easy to alphabetize the names on the list as it is to rearrange the record cards

C. *desirable*; this extra work with the record cards will give you more information about the patients

D. *undesirable*; adding an extra step to the procedure makes the work too complicated

10. Suppose that you have been given about two thousand 3x5 cards to arrange in numerical order. For you to sort the cards into broad groups, such as 1-100, 101-200, etc., and then arrange each group of cards in numerical order is

A. *desirable*; you will not be so apt to lose your place if interrupted when working with small groups of cards

B. *undesirable*; setting up a large number of groups of cards leads to more errors

C. *desirable*; the work can be done more quickly and easily with smaller groups of cards than with the entire group at once

D. *undesirable*; any procedure which requires so many steps wastes too much time

11. Of the following, the MOST important reason for keeping accurate records of clinic patients is that

A. these records provide valuable information for medical research purposes

B. accurate records are necessary to provide satisfactory medical care for the patients on return visits

C. complete records are necessary in order to prepare accurate and complete statistical reports on the work of the clinic

D. these records will show the large amount of work performed in the clinic

12. Suppose that one of the doctors who has been seeing patients on Wednesday changes his clinic day to Thursday. Two women who have previously had Wednesday appointments ask to come in on Thursday because they have great confidence in this doctor. For you to try to make Thursday appointments for them would be

A. *correct*; the wishes of the patients should be considered in making appointments

B. *wrong*; if the request were granted, the other patients would also want to have their appointments changed

C. *correct*; most patients would rather come to the clinic on Wednesdays

D. *wrong*; patients should not become too dependent upon any one physician

13. Of the following, the CHIEF reason for paying attention to a complaint from a clinic patient is that

A. government employees should always be courteous to the public

B. most people like to have others pay attention to their complaints

C. it does no harm to listen to complaints even if there is no merit to them

D. the patient may have good reason to complain

14. Assume that it is the rule in the clinic that the doctor is to sign the personal record card of each patient he examines. While you are filing the patients' record cards after the doctor has left the clinic, you notice that he has not signed the card of one of the patients he examined. Of the following, the MOST appropriate action for you to take is to

A. sign your own name on the card since the doctor has left the clinic

B. write the doctor's name on the card and sign your initials

C. file the unsigned card in the record file with the other cards

D. hold the card out and return it to the doctor for his signature on his next visit

14.___

15. Assume that it is the rule in the clinic that no patient may be seen after 4:00 P.M. so that the physicians and nurses will have time to write up cases and prepare for the following day. A few minutes after 4:00 P.M., an old woman who says she is in great pain and discomfort appears and asks for a doctor.
For you to try to arrange for a physician to see her is

A. *proper*; other patients waiting in the clinic will see how kind you are to sick people

B. *improper*; a rule should never be broken by public health personnel

C. *proper*; rules should not be interpreted too strictly when dealing with sick people

D. *improper*; the physician would be very annoyed if you disturbed him after 4:00 P.M.

15.___

16. Assume that you have been instructed to note on the record of each child who is vaccinated the lot number of the vaccine used.
Of the following, the MOST probable reason for this instruction is so that

A. a record can be kept of how much vaccine is used every year

B. if the child has an unfavorable reaction, the lot may be tested to determine the reason

C. no child will receive more than one vaccination

D. the oldest vaccine will be used first

16.___

17. The mother of a young child who is to be vaccinated against smallpox informs you that he gets hysterical at the sight of a needle.
Of the following, the BEST thing for you to do is to

A. assure the mother that the child's fears are groundless

B. speak to the child about the need to be protected against a serious disease like smallpox

17.___

C. tell the head nurse about the child's fear before he
is called for vaccination
D. promise the child a lollypop or toy if he behaves and
does not cry

18. A 10-year-old boy who is grossly overweight refuses to   18.___
remove any of his clothing before being weighed, apparently
because of embarrassment.
Of the following, it is BEST for you to
A. weigh him fully dressed and note this fact on the
record
B. insist that he remove his clothing since otherwise
the record would be inaccurate
C. note on the record card *grossly overweight*, as you
cannot weigh him with his clothing
D. ask the head nurse to use her authority to make the
boy undress

19. You notice that an 8-year-old boy who attends the clinic   19.___
stammers badly.
Of the following, it is BEST for you to
A. tell the doctor about his stammering in the boy's
presence
B. tell the boy each time you see him that his speech
has improved
C. ask the boy if he would like to go to a speech
correction clinic
D. make no reference to his stammer in the boy's presence

20. Of the following, the MOST important reason why you   20.___
should remain with a 4-year-old child when his temperature
is being taken by mouth is that otherwise the child might
A. fall off the chair and fracture an arm or leg
B. break the thermometer while it is in his mouth
C. remove the thermometer from his mouth and misplace it
D. leave the examining room and return to his mother

21. The BEST way to take the temperature of an infant is by   21.___
A. feeling his forehead
B. using an oral thermometer
C. placing a thermometer under his armpit
D. using a rectal thermometer

22. When the temperature of an adult is taken rectally, it is   22.___
LEAST accurate to say that the
A. temperature reading will be higher than if it were
taken orally
B. thermometer should be lubricated before use
C. thermometer should be in place for at least ten
minutes
D. temperature reading is likely to be more accurate
than if it were taken orally

23. When the temperature of an adult is taken orally, it is
    LEAST accurate to say that the

      A. thermometer should be washed with alcohol before it
    is used

      B. thermometer should be taken down below 96°F before
    it is used

      C. patient's temperature may be taken immediately after
    he has smoked a cigarette

      D. patient should be inactive just before his tempera-
    ture is taken

23.___

24. The nurse described the test to the patient before
    bringing him to the examining room for a basal metabolism
    test.
    Her action may BEST be described as

      A. *correct*; the patient will be more cooperative if he
    knows what to expect

      B. *wrong*; the nurse does not know how the test will
    affect the patient

      C. *correct*; the nurse can judge whether the patient is
    too upset by this information to take the test

      D. *wrong*; explaining the test beforehand will only make
    the patient nervous

24.___

25. When a patient's sputum test is *positive*, it means that
    the

      A. patient's sputum is plentiful

      B. doctor has made an accurate diagnosis

      C. patient has recovered and is now in good health

      D. laboratory reports that the patient's sputum contains
    certain disease germs

25.___

26. A biopsy can BEST be described as a(n)

      A. pre-cancerous condition B. examination of tissues
      C. living organism   D. germicidal solution

26.___

27. The *scratch* or *patch* test is usually given when testing
    for

      A. allergies   B. rheumatic fever
      C. blood poisoning   D. diabetes

27.___

28. Gamma globulin is frequently given to children after
    exposure to and before the appearance of symptoms of

      A. measles   B. smallpox
      C. tetanus   D. chickenpox

28.___

29. Of the following, the one which is NOT a respiratory
    disease is

      A. bronchitis   B. pneumonia
      C. nephritis   D. croup

29.___

30. A physician who specializes in the treatment of condi-
    tions affecting the skin is known as a

      A. urologist   B. dermatologist
      C. toxicologist   D. ophthalmologist

30.___

31. The branch of medicine which deals with diseases peculiar   31.___
    to women is
    A. pathology   B. orthopedics
    C. neurology   D. gynecology

32. The branch of medicine which deals with diseases of old   32.___
    age is called
    A. pediatrics   B. geriatrics
    C. serology   D. histology

33. *Petit mal* is a form of   33.___
    A. epilepsy   B. syphilis
    C. diabetes   D. malaria

34. Glaucoma is a disease of the   34.___
    A. thyroid gland   B. liver
    C. bladder   D. eye

35. A patient who has edema has   25.___
    A. not enough red blood cells
    B. too much water in the body tissues
    C. blood in the urine
    D. a swollen gland

36. The thoracic area of the body is located in the   36.___
    A. abdomen   B. lower back
    C. chest   D. neck

37. An electrocardiograph is MOST usually used in examination   37.___
    of the
    A. brain   B. heart
    C. kidney   D. gall bladder

38. The word *coagulate* means MOST NEARLY to   38.___
    A. bleed excessively   B. break up
    C. work together   D. form a clot

39. A stethoscope is used to examine the patient's   39.___
    A. heart   B. patellar reflex
    C. blood cells   D. spinal fluid

40. A pelvimeter is MOST usually used in the examination of   40.___
    a patient in the _____ clinic.
    A. chest   B. cancer   C. prenatal   D. eye

41. Tuberculin may BEST be described as a   41.___
    A. virus infection of the lungs
    B. preparation used in the diagnosis of tuberculosis
    C. sanitarium for tuberculous patients
    D. form of cancer of the lung

42. An autoclave is a(n)   42.____
    A. automatic dispenser of instruments needed for clinic
       examinations
    B. sterile place for storing clinic supplies until they
       are needed
    C. apparatus for sterilizing equipment under steam
       pressure
    D. portable self-operating general anesthesia unit

43. Radiation therapy is   43.____
    A. the recording of electrical impulses of the body on
       a graph
    B. a study of the effects of radiation fall-out on the
       human body
    C. a form of treatment used for certain diseases
    D. the filming of internal parts of the body through
       the use of x-rays

44. Diathermy is the treatment of patients by   44.____
    A. scientific use of baths and mineral waters
    B. insertion of radium into diseased tissues
    C. intravenous feedings of vitamins and minerals
    D. electrical generation of heat in the body tissues

45. The measurement of blood pressure involves two readings,   45.____
    which are known as _____ and _____.
    A. metabolic; diastolic   B. systolic; diastolic
    C. metabolic; hyperbolic   D. hyperbolic; systolic

46. The Snellen chart is used in examinations of the   46.____
    A. eyes   B. blood   C. urine   D. bile

47. An enema is MOST generally used to   47.____
    A. induce vomiting   B. irrigate the stomach
    C. clear the bowels   D. drain the urinary bladder

48. A bronchoscope is usually used in examinations of the   48.____
    A. kidneys   B. heart   C. stomach   D. lungs

49. The Wassermann test is used to find out if a patient has   49.____
    A. diphtheria   B. leukemia
    C. scarlet fever   D. syphilis

50. If a boiling water sterilizer is used, the minimum time   50.____
    necessary to sterilize instruments is MOST NEARLY _____
    hour(s).
    A. ½   B. 1   C. 1½   D. 2

51. To sterilize towels and dry gauze dressings in the health   51.____
    clinic, it is MOST advisable to
    A. dip them in a sterilizing solution
    B. wash them with a strong detergent
    C. boil them in the sterilizer
    D. steam them under pressure

52. Sterilization by use of chemicals rather than by boiling   52.____
water is indicated when the instrument
    A. is made of soft rubber
    B. has a sharp cutting edge
    C. has pus or blood on it
    D. was used more than 24 hours before sterilization

53. When dusting the furniture in the clinic, it is advisable   53.____
to use a silicone-treated dustcloth CHIEFLY because the
treated cloth will
    A. collect the dust more efficiently
    B. disinfect as well as dust the furniture
    C. not remove the wax from the furniture
    D. make it unnecessary to polish the furniture in the
       future

54. Assume that the clinic in which you work has issued   54.____
instructions that all supplies containing poison are to
have blue labels with the word *poison* clearly marked on
the label, and that these supplies are to be kept in a
storage cabinet separate from other supplies. You notice
that a bottle with no label is on a shelf in the *poison*
storage cabinet.
Of the following, the BEST action for you to take is to
    A. place the unlabeled bottle in the back of the regular
       storage cabinet
    B. put a blue label on the bottle and write *poison* on
       the label
    C. ask another public health employee to help you decide
       if the bottle contains poison
    D. pour the contents of the bottle into the slop sink
       and destroy the bottle

55. Assume that you have been assigned to care for the supply   55.____
room, and have been instructed to use the items which
have been in stock longest before using the newer stock.
Of the following, the MOST practical and time-saving way
to do this is to
    A. keep a record file of all supplies received and used
    B. write the dates when the supplies were received and
       used on the labels or containers
    C. place new supplies behind supplies of the same items
       already in stock
    D. keep the fastest moving stock in the most convenient
       places

56. The public health employee should know that clinic sup-   56.____
plies should be reordered
    A. as soon as the last container of the item in the
       supply closet is used up
    B. in the same amount on the first working day of each
       month
    C. whenever a let-up in clinic work makes time available
    D. when the records show that the stock may possibly be
       depleted within a month

57. The CHIEF reason for storing x-ray film in lead containers 57.____
is that lead containers protect the film from
    A. moisture in the atmosphere
    B. exposure to stray x-rays
    C. dust and other particles
    D. extreme changes in temperature

58. You have been instructed to keep all narcotics locked in 58.____
a separate cabinet when storing supplies.
The one of the following which should be kept locked in
this cabinet is a preparation containing
    A. cortisone B. codeine   C. caffeine   D. quinine

59. Of the following medical supplies, the one which should 59.____
be refrigerated is
    A. vaseline jelly   B. paregoric
    C. aureomycin   D. aspirin tablets

60. The one of the following which is NOT an antiseptic or 60.____
disinfectant is
    A. distilled water   B. alcohol
    C. lysol   D. hydrogen peroxide

61. The one of the following which is an anesthetic is 61.____
    A. novocaine   B. phenobarbital
    C. benzedrine   D. witch hazel

62. The wide use of antibiotics has presented a number of 62.____
problems. Some patients become allergic to the drugs so
that they cannot be used when they are needed. In other
cases, after prolonged treatment with antibiotics,
certain organisms no longer respond to them at all. This
is one of the reasons for the constant search for more
potent drugs.
On the basis of this paragraph, the one of the following
statements which is MOST NEARLY correct is that
    A. antibiotics have been used successfully for certain
       allergies
    B. antibiotics should never be used for prolonged treat-
       ment
    C. because they have developed an allergy to the drug,
       antibiotics cannot be used when needed for certain
       patients
    D. one of the reasons for the constant search for new
       antibiotics is that so many diseases have been
       successfully treated with these drugs

63. The over-use of antibiotics today represents a growing 63.____
danger, according to many medical authorities. Patients
everywhere, stimulated by reports of new wonder drugs,
continue to ask their doctors for a shot to relieve a
cold, grippe, or any of the other virus infections that
occur during the course of a bad winter. But, for the
common cold and many other virus infections, antibiotics
have no effect.

On the basis of this paragraph, the one of the following statements which is MOST NEARLY correct is that
  A. the use of antibiotics is becoming a health hazard
  B. antibiotics are of no value in the treatment of many virus infections
  C. patients should ask their doctors for a shot of one of the new wonder drugs to relieve the symptoms of grippe
  D. the treatment of colds and other virus infections by antibiotics will lessen their severity

64. Statistics tell us that heart disease kills more people than any other illness, and the death rate still continues to rise. People over 30 have a fifty-fifty chance of escaping, for heart disease is chiefly an illness of people in late middle age and advanced years. Because there are more people in this age group living today than there were some years ago, heart disease is able to find more victims.
On the basis of this paragraph, the one of the following statements which is MOST NEARLY correct is that
  A. half of the people over 30 years of age have heart disease today
  B. more people die of heart disease than of all other diseases combined
  C. older people are the chief victims of heart disease
  D. the rising birth rate has increased the possibility that the average person will die of heart disease

64.___

65. There is evidence that some individuals, given three doses of polio vaccine, have not developed enough immunity to protect themselves against paralytic polio. It is thought that immunity will be increased by a fourth injection given no sooner than one year after the third injection and many health agencies have been giving a fourth injection to their patients.
On the basis of this paragraph, the one of the following statements which is MOST NEARLY correct is that
  A. three doses of polio vaccine will not give any protection from paralytic polio
  B. a fourth injection of polio vaccine guarantees immunity to polio
  C. the fourth injection of polio vaccine should be given as soon as possible after the third injection
  D. the fourth injection of polio vaccine should be given at least a year after the third injection

65.___

Questions 66-72.

DIRECTIONS: Questions 66 through 72 are to be answered on the basis of the following table.

REPORT ON PATIENTS ATTENDING SELECTED HEALTH CLINICS January to December (This Year)					
CLINICS	A	B	C	D	E
Child Health	62,400	70,200	81,900	83,400	22,300
Chest	53,300	52,000	64,800	47,600	4,500
Social Hygiene	24,500	21,900	18,400	13,500	4,100
Eye	10,600	12,600	13,300	13,800	4,200
Cardiac	1,400	1,600	1,700	1,300	400
Prenatal	1,300	1,800	1,700	1,800	500

66. On the basis of the above chart, the group with the LARGEST number of patients attending the eye clinics was

    A. B   B. C   C. A   D. D

66.____

67. If the population of the area located around group E was 210,000, the percentage of this population who attended the eye clinic was MOST NEARLY

    A. .02%   B. 2%   C. 5%   D. 21%

67.____

68. If the clinics were open 250 days, the average daily attendance at the social hygiene clinics in group C was MOST NEARLY

    A. 74   B. 88   C. 259   D. 736

68.____

69. The percentage of all patients attending group E clinics who attended the chest clinics was MOST NEARLY

    A. 5%   B. 8%   C. 13%   D. 25%

69.____

70. If 25% of the patients attending prenatal clinics in group B also attended the cardiac clinics, the number of prenatal clinic patients in group B who did NOT attend the cardiac clinics was MOST NEARLY

    A. 400   B. 450   C. 1200   D. 1350

70.____

71. If the number of persons who attended all clinics in group A last year was 20% less than this year, the number who attended the group A clinics last year was MOST NEARLY

    A. 32,700   B. 130,800   C. 163,500   D. 196,200

71.____

72. Assume that at the end of the year it was found that half of the people who attended the group B chest clinics had been found to be free of disease, 1/3 were discharged as needing no further care, and the rest were instructed to return to the clinic for further treatment.
The number of persons who were told to return for further treatment was MOST NEARLY

    A. 7,000   B. 14,000   C. 21,000   D. 35,000

72.____

Questions 73-84.

DIRECTIONS: Each of Questions 73 through 84 consists of a word, in capitals, followed by four suggested meanings of the word. For each question, indicate in the space at the right the letter preceding the word which means MOST NEARLY the same as the word in capitals.

73. PUNCTUAL   73.____
    A. usual   B. hollow
    C. infrequent   D. on time

74. BENEFICIAL   74.____
    A. popular   B. forceful   C. helpful   D. necessary

75. TEMPORARY   75.____
    A. permanently   B. for a limited time
    C. at the same time   D. frequently

76. INQUIRE   76.____
    A. order   B. agree   C. ask   D. discharge

77. SUFFICIENT   77.____
    A. enough   B. inadequate
    C. thorough   D. capable

78. AMBULATORY   78.____
    A. bedridden   B. lefthanded
    C. walking   D. laboratory

79. DILATE   79.____
    A. enlarge   B. contract   C. revise   D. restrict

80. NUTRITIOUS   80.____
    A. protective   B. healthful
    C. fattening   D. nourishing

81. CONGENITAL   81.____
    A. with pleasure   B. defective
    C. likeable   D. existing from birth

82. ISOLATION   82.____
    A. sanitation   B. quarantine
    C. rudeness   D. exposure

83. SPASM   83.____
    A. splash   B. twitch   C. space   D. blow

84. HEMORRHAGE   84.____
    A. bleeding   B. ulcer
    C. hereditary disease   D. lack of blood

Questions 85-90.

DIRECTIONS: Questions 85 through 90 are to be answered on the basis
of the usual rules for alphabetical filing. For each
question, indicate in the space at the right the
letter preceding the name which should be filed THIRD
in alphabetical order.

85. A. Hesselberg, Norman J.   B. Hesselman, Nathan B.   85.____
     C. Hazel, Robert S.   D. Heintz, August J.

86. A. Oshins, Jerome   B. Ohsie, Marjorie   86.____
     C. O'Shaugn, F.J.   D. O'Shea, Frances

87. A. Petrie, Joshua A.   B. Pendleton, Oscar   87.____
     C. Pertweee, Joshua   D. Perkins, Warren G.

88. A. Morganstern, Alfred   B. Morganstern, Albert   88.____
     C. Monroe, Mildred   D. Modesti, Ernest

89. A. More, Stewart   B. Moorhead, Jay   89.____
     C. Moore, Benjamin   D. Moffat, Edith

90. A. Ramirez, Paul   B. Revere, Pauline   90.____
     C. Ramos, Felix   D. Ramazotti, Angelo

Questions 91-100.

DIRECTIONS: Questions 91 through 100 are to be answered on the basis
of the usual rules of filing. Column I lists the names
of 10 clinic patients. Column II lists the headings of
file drawers into which you are to place the records of
these patients. For each question, indicate in the
space at the right the letter preceding the heading of
the file drawer in which the record should be filed.

	COLUMN I	COLUMN II	
91.	Charles Coughlin	A. Cab-Cep	91.____
92.	Mary Carstairs	B. Ceq-Cho	92.____
93.	Joseph Collin	C. Chr-Coj	93.____
94.	Thomas Chelsey	D. Cok-Czy	94.____
95.	Cedric Chalmers		95.____
96.	Mae Clarke		96.____
97.	Dora Copperhead		97.____
98.	Arnold Cohn		98.____
99.	Charlotte Crumboldt		99.____
100.	Frances Celine		100.____

KEY (CORRECT ANSWERS)

1. B	21. D	41. B	61. A	81. D
2. C	22. C	42. C	62. C	82. B
3. A	23. C	43. C	63. B	83. B
4. C	24. A	44. D	64. C	84. A
5. A	25. D	45. B	65. D	85. A
6. D	26. B	46. A	66. D	86. D
7. B	27. A	47. C	67. B	87. C
8. D	28. A	48. D	68. A	88. B
9. A	29. C	49. D	69. C	89. B
10. C	30. B	50. A	70. D	90. C
11. B	31. D	51. D	71. B	91. D
12. A	32. B	52. B	72. A	92. A
13. D	33. A	53. A	73. D	93. D
14. D	34. D	54. D	74. C	94. B
15. C	35. B	55. C	75. B	95. B
16. B	36. C	56. D	76. C	96. C
17. C	37. B	57. B	77. A	97. D
18. A	38. D	58. B	78. C	98. C
19. D	39. A	59. C	79. A	99. D
20. B	40. C	60. A	80. D	100. A

EXAMINATION SECTION
TEST 1

DIRECTIONS: Each question or incomplete statement is followed by several suggested answers or completions. Select the one that BEST answers the question or completes the statement. *PRINT THE LETTER OF THE CORRECT ANSWER IN THE SPACE AT THE RIGHT.*

1. Of the following, the MOST important reason for requiring that an employee have knowledge of medical office procedures is that   1.___
   A. she can take care of sick people in the absence of a doctor
   B. patients in the clinic will be impressed with her apparent knowledge
   C. she will be more helpful in her work at the clinic
   D. letters she may have to write will be more concise

2. A newly appointed employee should have a good understanding of her functions in the Department of Health.   2.___
   Of the following, the training which would be LEAST helpful to her in the performance of her functions is
   A. an understanding of the role of the Department of Health in the community
   B. development of skill in the technics of work in a health center
   C. information as to the services offered in the health center
   D. development of skill in the care of the sick in their own homes

3. If an employee were called upon at the same time to attend to each of the following, the one she should do FIRST is   3.___
   A. sterilize instruments used in the examination of the last patient
   B. answer the telephone
   C. give the patient who is just leaving another appointment
   D. check to see if a patient who has just arrived has an appointment

4. Of the following, the LEAST important reason for answering telephone calls promptly in the health clinic is that   4.___
   A. patients waiting in the clinic will be impressed with the self-importance of the employee
   B. patients calling for information will be answered quickly
   C. the public will get a favorable impression of the Department of Health
   D. it will result in better service by keeping the lines free for other calls

5. Assume that the physician assigned to the clinic in which   5.___
   you work calls the clinic and tells you that he has been
   detained for half an hour and will not be able to report
   at 1:00 P.M. as scheduled.
   You should
   A. not say anything about the call to anyone
   B. report this information to your immediate supervisor
   C. tell the patient scheduled for 1:00 P.M. to come back
      the next day
   D. tell the physician that he must come at 1:00 P.M.
      since a patient has been scheduled for that time

6. Assume that a physician who is examining a patient asks   6.___
   you to hand him a certain instrument from the tray. You
   do not know exactly what he is referring to.
   The BEST thing for you to do is to
   A. give him an instrument which you think might be
      suitable for the examination
   B. ask him to repeat what he said
   C. admit that you cannot identify the instrument he wants
   D. tell him that there is no such instrument on the tray

7. Assume that a patient asks you to explain something the   7.___
   doctor told her about her illness which she says she does
   not understand.
   For you to suggest that she tell the doctor that she did
   not understand what he told her and ask him to explain it
   again is
   A. *advisable*; the patient will be impressed by your
      interest in her
   B. *inadvisable*; patients get tired of the run-around
   C. *advisable*; the doctor is best qualified to answer
      questions concerning or affecting the patient's health
   D. *inadvisable*; the patient will lose confidence in your
      ability

8. Assume that, after you have been employed for several   8.___
   months, the nurse who is your immediate supervisor summons
   you to her office. She tells you that she has noticed
   on several occasions that you have been careless about
   your personal appearance.
   In this instance, it would be
   A. proper for you to tell her that your personal appear-
      ance is no concern of hers
   B. advisable for you to listen politely to her and then
      do nothing about it
   C. fitting for you to tell her that the other employees
      in the clinic are just as careless
   D. best for you to thank her for her interest and to tell
      her that you will make an effort to be more careful

9. One of the patients at the Health Center insists that she   9.___
    be sent to a different doctor as she does not like the
    doctor she saw last week.
    Of the following answers, the one that is MOST advisable
    for you to give to the patient is that
    A. she will have to take whatever doctor is available
    B. all the clinic doctors are equally good
    C. you will try to send her to another doctor
    D. she should see the nurse in charge

10. Suppose that the doctor in the clinic has given you an   10.___
    order which is contrary to the usual clinic procedure.
    Of the following, the BEST action for you to take is to
    A. point out to the doctor the usual clinic procedure
       and then do as he tells you
    B. refuse to do what he tells you as it is contrary to
       the usual procedure
    C. refuse to do what he tells you and call the nurse in
       charge
    D. do as the doctor tells you and at the first oppor-
       tunity report the occurrence to the nurse in charge

11. When filing some patients' record cards in an alphabetic   11.___
    file, you notice that one card obviously has been mis-
    filed.
    In this case, it would be MOST advisable for you to
    A. pay no attention to this as you believe it was not
       your error
    B. pull out the card and file it correctly
    C. report this to the clinic supervisor and suggest to
       her that she reprimand the employee who you believe
       is responsible for the misfiling
    D. take no particular care in the future when filing
       cards since errors will occur anyway

12. Assume that you are working directly with children in a   12.___
    well baby clinic. You feel feverish.
    Of the following, the BEST action for you to take is to
    A. wait and see whether you feel better; you don't want
       to seem to be a chronic complainer
    B. report immediately to the nurse in charge that you
       do not feel well
    C. take your temperature and, if it is over 101°F,
       report to the nurse in charge
    D. report to the nurse in charge only if you have other
       symptoms

13. As a receptionist in a public health center, you have   13.___
    certain responsibilities towards patients and other
    callers. You should greet each caller promptly and
    courteously. Never keep a caller waiting while you carry
    on a personal conversation, either on the telephone or
    with another employee. However, if you are occupied with
    clinic matters, give the caller to understand that you
    will be with him in a short while.

On the basis of this paragraph, if a caller comes in while you are discussing with the nurse in charge coverage of the clinic during the lunch hour, the one of the following actions which would be the BEST for you to take is to
    A. stop and take care of his needs immediately as you should never keep a caller waiting
    B. nod to him and continue making plans for clinic coverage
    C. say to him that you will take care of him in a moment; then finish making your plans for clinic coverage
    D. finish making plans for clinic coverage with the nurse in charge and then inquire into the caller's needs

14. Assume that you are responsible for scheduling clinic appointments. One of the patients who has to report to the clinic every Tuesday morning asks that his appointments be scheduled for the last half hour of the clinic session. It has been the practice in this clinic to keep the last half hour open only for emergency appointments, and to schedule all appointments in order, from the time when the clinic opens.
Of the following, the BEST action for you to take is to
    A. schedule the appointment at the time requested by the patient as he probably has a good reason for wanting it then
    B. disregard his request as no one attending a clinic should be given special consideration
    C. deny his request unless he has a medical reason for asking for a late appointment
    D. refer the request to the nurse in charge to determine if he should be given a late appointment

  14.____

15. Suppose that a patient who is registered in the Social Hygiene Clinic of a Health Center appears in a drunken condition for a scheduled appointment.
Of the following, the BEST action for you to take is to
    A. inform the nurse in charge of the situation
    B. have him await his turn with the other patients
    C. send him home, telling him not to return until he is sober
    D. arrange for him to see the doctor immediately

  15.____

16. Assume that you have been asked by your supervisor to instruct a newly-appointed aide in the performance of a given task.
Of the following, the BEST procedure for you to follow is
    A. to check her work only once after you have shown her how to do it; continued supervision after this should be the supervisor's responsibility
    B. not to check her work after you have shown her how to do it as she may resent your supervision
    C. not to check her work immediately but wait until she has done the task several times in order to give her a fair chance

  16.____

D. to check her work at frequent intervals after you have
shown her how to do it until she is able to perform
the given task

17. A worker should be carefully introduced to the clinic to   17.___
which she has been assigned. The period of orientation
will vary widely with the individual, her previous experience, and the type of clinic to which she is assigned.
In general, it will include an introduction to the physical set-up, the personnel, the type of service to be
rendered, and the ideals of the clinic. In the beginning,
the new worker should be given simple assignments and
close supervision. The program should be arranged so as
to give the nurse in charge opportunity to study the
worker as to personality, general ability, or any special
handicaps.
According to this paragraph, the one of the following
statements that is MOST accurate is that, during the first
few days, the new worker should
   A. do nothing but observe the physical set-up, the
      personnel, the type of service rendered, the ideals
      of the clinic
   B. be given a 30 hour course in the clinic to which she
      is assigned, including the physical set-up, the
      personnel, the ideals of the clinic
   C. be observed by the nurse in charge as to her ability
      to do the work in the clinic to which she has been
      assigned
   D. be closely supervised by the nurse in charge until
      she has a thorough knowledge of the clinic

18. Preparing a patient for physical examination has impor-   18.___
tant mental aspects. Because each patient is individual
in his reactions, a worker must plan her approach so as
to deal with these reactions sympathetically. Thus,
one patient may be afraid of the pain an examination may
cause him immediately, another may fear that he will have
unpleasant effects later, and still another may be only
curious about the examination and have neither fear nor
anxiety.
On the basis of this paragraph, the one of the following
statements that BEST describes the reactions of patients
when undergoing examination is that all patients
   A. are afraid when being examined
   B. react differently to an examination
   C. are afraid of the after-effects of an examination
   D. are curious about the examination

19. A recently published article states: Weight for height   19.___
and age is, as many have previously held, an inadequate
index of the *nutritional status* of a child. It is un-
scientific and unfair to set average weight as a goal
for all children or for an individual child. Weighing
and measuring, however, should be continued as a record
of the trend of individual growth which is of value to
the physician in relation to other findings and as
valuable devices to interest the child in his growth.

According to this article, weighing and measuring the
height of children
   A. are of no value and should be stopped
   B. are useful to the physician
   C. are of no value but give interesting information
   D. indicate the nutritional status of the child

20. Blood pressure is the force that the blood exerts against   20.___
    the walls of the vessels through which it flows. The
    blood pressure is commonly meant to be the pressure in
    the arteries. The pressure in the arteries varies with
    the contraction (work period) and the relaxation (rest
    period) of the heart. When the heart contracts, the
    blood in the arteries is at its greatest pressure. This
    is called the systolic pressure. When the heart relaxes,
    the blood in the arteries is at its lowest pressure.
    This is called the diastolic pressure. The difference
    between both pressures is called the pulse pressure.
    The one of the following statements that is MOST accurate
    on the basis of this paragraph is that
       A. the blood in the arteries is at its greatest pressure
          during contraction
       B. systolic pressure measures the blood in the arteries
          when the heart is relaxed
       C. blood pressure is determined by obtaining the
          difference between systolic and diastolic pressure
       D. pulse pressure is the same as blood pressure

21. Lymph is a clear fluid, rich in white blood cells, and   21.___
    is actually blood plasma which has filtered through the
    walls of capillaries. It is circulated through the lymph
    vessels and in all the tissue spaces of the body. It
    carries nourishment and oxygen to the tissues and waste
    products away from them.
    The one of the following statements that is NOT correct
    on the basis of this paragraph is that lymph
       A. contains red blood cells
       B. contains white blood cells
       C. is a basic part of blood
       D. is circulated through the body

22. When storing medical supplies, it is important to remember   22.___
    that liquids should be labeled
       A. only if the liquids are poisonous and there is the
          slightest chance that they will not be recognized
       B. whenever there is the slightest chance that they
          will not be recognized
       C. at all times, and discarded if labels have become
          detached
       D. only in those cases where the liquids will be given
          to patients

23. When dusting metal countertops in the clinic, it is BEST   23.___
to use a clean cloth which is
    A. medicated   B. wet   C. dry   D. damp

24. Of the following statements concerning a hypodermic   24.___
syringe, the one that is MOST correct is that a plunger
    A. used for taking blood specimens can be used with any
       syringe barrel
    B. can be used for any syringe barrel as long as it
       goes in easily
    C. can be used only with the syringe barrel that was
       made for it
    D. must be used with the syringe barrel that was made
       for it only if it is to be used for injections

25. The one of the following which should NOT be done when   25.___
using a thermometer is to
    A. shake down the thermometer to 95°F before taking the
       patient's temperature
    B. ask the patient to keep his lips closed when taking
       the temperature orally
    C. wash the thermometer in hot soapy water after use
    D. keep the thermometer in a container of alcohol when
       not in use

26. The temperature of an adult when taken by rectum is   26.___
usually _____ than if taken _____ under the armpit.
    A. *higher*; either by mouth or
    B. *higher*; by mouth and lower than if taken
    C. *lower*; either by mouth or
    D. *lower*; by mouth and higher if taken

27. Of the following tests, the one which is associated   27.___
with tuberculosis is the _____ test.
    A. Schick   B. Mantoux   C. Dick   D. Kahn

28. A needle that has been used to draw blood should be   28.___
rinsed immediately after use in
    A. a disinfectant solution   B. hot water
    C. cold water   D. hot, soapy water

29. Of the following, the statement that is MOST correct is   29.___
that a hypodermic needle should be checked for burrs,
hooks, and sharpness
    A. once a week
    B. before it is sterilized
    C. after it has been sterilized
    D. after it has been used three or four times

30. The MOST accurate of the following statements is that,   30.___
when a syringe and needle are being sterilized by boiling, the
    A. plunger must be completely out of the barrel
    B. needle should be left attached to the barrel as when
       in use

    C. plunger may be completely inside the barrel
    D. needle should be boiled at least twice as long as
       the syringe

31. Of the following, the MOST important reason for washing   31.___
    an instrument in hot soapy water is to
    A. sterilize the instrument
    B. destroy germs by heat
    C. destroy germs by coagulation
    D. remove foreign matter and bacteria

32. Assume that a hypodermic needle which is to be used for   32.___
    injection is accidentally brushed at the tip by your hand.
    Of the following, the action which should be taken before
    this needle is used is that it be
    A. washed under the hot water tap
    B. wiped with a sterile piece of gauze
    C. washed in hot soapy water, then rinsed in sterile
       water
    D. boiled for ten minutes

33. The CORRECT way to sterilize a scalpel is to   33.___
    A. place it in a chemical germicide
    B. boil it for 10 minutes
    C. put it in the autoclave
    D. pass it through a bright flame

34. Assume that a tray of instruments has been accidentally   34.___
    left uncovered for five minutes after it had been
    sterilized.
    Of the following, the action you should take to ensure
    that the instruments are sterile for use is to
    A. dip them in boiling water
    B. boil them for 10 minutes
    C. replace the cover on the tray
    D. wipe each instrument with sterile gauze

35. An intramuscular injection is MOST likely to be used in   35.___
    the administration of
    A. smallpox vaccine   B. streptomycin
    C. glucose   D. blood

36. The one of the following which is NOT a normal element   36.___
    of blood is
    A. hemoglobin   B. a leucocyte
    C. marrow   D. a platelet

37. Of the following statements regarding the Salk vaccine,   37.___
    the MOST accurate one is that it
    A. immunizes children and adults against paralytic
       poliomyelitis
    B. is a test to determine the presence of poliomyelitis
       virus in the blood

    C. is a test to determine whether a child is immune to
       poliomyelitis
    D. is used in the treatment of patients suffering from
       paralytic poliomyelitis

38. The GREATEST success in the treatment of cancer has been   38.___
    in cancer of the
    A. blood   B. stomach   C. liver   D. skin

39. An autopsy is a(n)   39.___
    A. type of blood test
    B. examination of tissue removed from a living organism
    C. examination of a human body after death
    D. test to determine the acidity of body fluids

40. The word *vascular* is MOST closely associated with   40.___
    A. the circulatory system   B. respiration
    C. digestion   D. the nervous system

41. The word *diagnosis* means MOST NEARLY   41.___
    A. preparation of a diagram
    B. determination of an illness
    C. medical examination of a patient
    D. written prescription

42. A tendon connects   42.___
    A. bone to bone   B. muscle to bone
    C. muscle to muscle   D. muscle to ligament

43. Blood takes on oxygen as it passes through the   43.___
    A. liver   B. heart   C. spleen   D. lungs

44. The fatty substance in the blood which is deposited in   44.___
    the artery walls and which is believed to cause hardening
    of the arteries is called
    A. amino acid   B. phenol
    C. cholesterol   D. pectin

45. The digestive canal includes the   45.___
    A. stomach, small intestine, large intestine, and rectum
    B. stomach, larynx, large intestine, and rectum
    C. trachea, small intestine, large intestine, and rectum
    D. stomach, small intestine, large intestine, and
       abdominal cavity

46. When giving artificial respiration, it should be kept in   46.___
    mind that air is drawn into the lungs by the
    A. expansion of the chest cavity
    B. contraction of the chest cavity
    C. expansion of the lungs
    D. contraction of the lungs

47. The formula for converting degrees Centigrade to degrees   47.___
    Fahrenheit is as follows:
          Fahrenheit = 9/5 of Centigrade + 32°, or
          (multiply the number of degrees Centigrade by 9,
              divide by 5 and add 32)
    If the Centigrade thermometer reads 25°, the temperature,
    in degrees Fahrenheit, is
          A. 13   B. 45   C. 53   D. 77

48. To make a certain preparation, you have been told to mix   48.___
    one ounce of Liquid A and 3 ounces of Liquid B.
    If you have used 18 ounces of Liquid B in preparing a
    larger amount, the number of ounces of Liquid A you
    should use is
          A. 6   B. 15   C. 21   D. 54

49. If one inch is equal to approximately 2.5 centimeters,   49.___
    the number of inches in fifteen centimeters is MOST
    NEARLY
          A. 1.6   B. 6   C. 12.5   D. 37.5

Questions 50-52.

DIRECTIONS: Questions 50 through 52 are to be answered on the
              basis of the following situation.

*You have been asked to keep records of the time spent with
each patient by the doctors in the clinic where you are assigned.
Your notes show that Dr. Jones spent the following amount of time
with each patient he examined on a certain day:*
          Patient A - 14 minutes; Patient B - 13 minutes;
          Patient C - 34 minutes; Patient D - 48 minutes;
          Patient E - 26 minutes; Patient F - 20 minutes;
          Patient G - 25 minutes.

50. The average number of minutes spent by Dr. Jones with   50.___
    each patient is MOST NEARLY
          A. 20   B. 25   C. 30   D. 35

51. If Dr. Jones is to take care of the seven patients men-   51.___
    tioned above at one session, the number of hours he will
    have to remain at the clinic is MOST NEARLY _____ hour(s).
          A. 1   B. 2   C. 3   D. 4

52. The one of the following groups of patients that required   52.___
    the LEAST time to be examined is Patients
          A. A, C, and E   B. B, D, and F
          C. C, E, and G   D. A, D, and G

Questions 53-60.

DIRECTIONS: Questions 53 through 60 are to be answered on the basis of the usual rules of filing. Column I lists the names of 8 clinic patients. Column II lists the headings of file drawers into which you are to place the records of these patients. In the space at the right, corresponding to the names in Column I, print the letter preceding the heading of the file drawer in which the record should be filed.

COLUMN I	COLUMN II	
53. Thomas Adams	A. Aab-Abi	53.___
54. Joseph Albert	B. Abj-Ach	54.___
55. Frank Anaster	C. Aci-Aco	55.___
56. Charles Abt	D. Acp-Ada	56.___
57. John Alfred	E. Adb-Afr	57.___
58. Louis Aron	F. Afs-Ago	58.___
59. Francis Amos	G. Agp-Ahz	59.___
60. William Adler	H. Aia-Ako	60.___
	I. Akp-Ald	
	J. Ale-Amo	
	K. Amp-Aor	
	L. Aos-Apr	
	M. Aps-Asi	
	N. Asj-Ati	
	O. Atj-Awz	

Questions 61-66.

DIRECTIONS: In answering Questions 61 through 66, alphabetize the four names listed in each question; then print in the space at the right the four letters preceding the alphabetized names to show the CORRECT alphabetical arrangement of the four names.

61. A. Frank Adam   B. Frank Aarons   61.___
    C. Frank Aaron   D. Frank Adams

62. A. Richard Lavine   B. Richard Levine   62.___
    C. Edward Lawrence   D. Edward Loraine

63. A. G. Frank Adam   B. Frank Adam   63.___
    C. Fanny Adam   D. Franklin Adam

64. A. George Cohn   B. Richard Cohen   64.___
    C. Thomas Cohane   D. George Cohan

65. A. Paul Shultz   B. Robert Schmid   65.___
    C. Joseph Schwartz   D. Edward Schmidt

66. A. Peter Consilazio   B. Frank Consolezio   66.___
    C. Robert Consalizio   D. Ella Consolizio

Questions 67-80.

DIRECTIONS: For Questions 67 through 80, select the letter preceding the word which means MOST NEARLY the same as the word in capital letters.

67. LEGIBLE   67.___
    A. readable   B. eligible   C. learned   D. lawful

68. OBSERVE   68.___
    A. assist   B. watch   C. correct   D. oppose

69. HABITUAL   69.___
    A. punctual   B. occasional
    C. usual   D. actual

70. CHRONOLOGICAL   70.___
    A. successive   B. earlier
    C. later   D. studious

71. ARREST   71.___
    A. punish   B. run   C. threaten   D. stop

72. ABSTAIN   72.___
    A. refrain   B. indulge   C. discolor   D. spoil

73. TOXIC   73.___
    A. poisonous   B. decaying
    C. taxing   D. defective

74. TOLERATE   74.___
    A. fear   B. forgive   C. allow   D. despise

75. VENTILATE   75.___
    A. vacate   B. air   C. extricate   D. heat

76. SUPERIOR   76.___
    A. perfect   B. subordinate
    C. lower   D. higher

77. EXTREMITY   77.___
    A. extent   B. limb   C. illness   D. execution

78. DIVULGED   78.___
    A. unrefined   B. secreted
    C. revealed   D. divided

79. SIPHON   79.___
    A. drain   B. drink   C. compute   D. discard

80. EXPIRATION   80.___
    A. trip   B. demonstration
    C. examination   D. end

Questions 81-100.

DIRECTIONS: Column I lists 20 words, numbered 81 through 100, which
             are used in medical practice. Column II lists words or
             phrases which describe the words in Column I. In the
             space at the right, next to the number of each of the
             words in Column I, place the letter preceding the words
             or phrases in Column II which BEST describes the word
             in Column I.

COLUMN I   COLUMN II

81. Anemia   A. A tube used to drain fluid   81.___
                             from the bladder
82. Anesthetic   82.___
                          B. The skull
83. Arthritis   83.___
                          C. Inflammation of a joint
84. Aseptic   84.___
                          D. A fluid injected into the
85. Astigmatism   rectum for the purpose of   85.___
                             clearing out the bowels
86. Catheter   86.___
                          E. A drug used in surgery which
87. Cranium   makes one insensible to pain   87.___

88. Diathermy   F. Rheumatic pain in the back   88.___

89. Enema   G. The branch of medicine con-   89.___
                             cerned with diseases of the
90. Electrocardiograph   eye   90.___

91. Forceps   H. Examination of the inner parts 91.___
                             of the body by use of x-rays
92. Gynecology   and a special screen   92.___

COLUMN I	COLUMN II	
93. Lesion	I. Free from disease germs	93.___
94. Lumbago	J. Deficiency of blood	94.___
95. Microscope	K. The branch of medicine concerned with diseases of women	95.___
96. Obstetrics		96.___
97. Ophthalmology	L. A tumorous growth	97.___
98. Postnatal	M. A structural defect of the eye	98.___
99. Rabies	N. An apparatus for sterilization under pressurized steam	99.___
100. Stethoscope	O. The shoulder blade	100.___

P. A type of treatment which depends upon production of heat in the tissues by high frequency current

Q. An instrument for recording electric changes caused by contraction of the muscles of the heart

R. An instrument for magnifying minute organisms

S. The branch of medicine concerned with the care and delivery of pregnant women

T. A wound or injury

U. An acute infectious disease which is transmitted by the bite of dogs and other animals

V. A band of tissue which connects bones or holds organs in place

W. A medication used to calm nerves

X. An instrument used to listen to sounds in the heart

Y. A pair of tongs

Z. Occurring after birth

KEY (CORRECT ANSWERS)

1. C	26. A	51. C	76. D
2. D	27. B	52. A	77. B
3. B	28. C	53. D	78. C
4. A	29. B	54. I	79. A
5. B	30. A	55. K	80. D
6. C	31. D	56. B	81. J
7. C	32. D	57. J	82. E
8. D	33. A	58. M	83. C
9. D	34. B	59. J	84. I
10. A	35. B	60. E	85. M
11. B	36. C	61. C,B,A,D	86. A
12. B	37. A	62. A,C,B,D	87. B
13. C	38. D	63. C,B,D,A	88. P
14. D	39. C	64. D,C,B,A	89. D
15. A	40. A	65. B,D,C,A	90. Q
16. D	41. B	66. C,A,B,D	91. Y
17. C	42. B	67. A	92. K
18. B	43. D	68. B	93. T
19. B	44. C	69. C	94. F
20. A	45. A	70. A	95. R
21. A	46. A	71. D	96. S
22. C	47. D	72. A	97. G
23. D	48. A	73. A	98. Z
24. C	49. B	74. C	99. U
25. C	50. B	75. B	100. X

EXAMINATION SECTION
TEST 1

DIRECTIONS: Each question or incomplete statement is followed by several suggested answers or completions. Select the one that BEST answers the question or completes the statement. *PRINT THE LETTER OF THE CORRECT ANSWER IN THE SPACE AT THE RIGHT.*

1. The use of a solution of boiling water and bicarbonate of soda for sterilizing scalpels and other cutting instruments is
   A. *advisable*; all germs and bacteria will be efficiently removed from the instruments
   B. *inadvisable*; this process would dull the cutting edges of the instruments
   C. *advisable*; this procedure eliminates the necessity for washing soiled instruments
   D. *inadvisable*; boiling tends to rust these instruments

1.___

2. The autoclave is a(n)
   A. apparatus for sterilizing under pressure
   B. automatic stomach pump
   C. portable self-operating general anesthesia unit
   D. self-adjusting leg-splint

2.___

3. The MOST accurate of the following statements with regard to a patient's pulse is that
   A. the pulse should be taken by pressing the thumb against the artery on the wrist
   B. the pulse rate is not ordinarily affected by excitement or other emotional experiences
   C. the average normal pulse rate is 120-140 beats per minute
   D. in cases of severe shock, the pulse may become very rapid and weak

3.___

4. Incontinency is the term used to describe
   A. involuntary passage of urine
   B. nosebleed
   C. inflammation of a nerve
   D. a mild form of insanity

4.___

5. A biopsy is BEST described as a(n)
   A. post-mortem examination of a human body
   B. blood test
   C. examination of tissue removed from a living organism
   D. test to determine acidity of body fluids

5.___

6. Dyspepsia is BEST described as a condition in which there is
   A. great difficulty in breathing
   B. a disturbance of digestion
   C. lack of energy due to insufficient food
   D. an uncontrollable desire for alcoholic beverages

6.___

7. Hematology is the science concerned with the composition   7.___
    and function of
    A. blood   B. bile
    C. spinal fluid   D. gastric juice

8. The name of the test which is used to indicate immunity   8.___
    from or susceptibility to diphtheria is
    A. Snellen   B. Dick
    C. Wassermann   D. Schick

9. The one of the following which is a part of the nervous   9.___
    system is the
    A. spinal cord   B. pancreas
    C. muscle   D. cranium

10. Bacteria are known to flourish BEST in a place which is   10.___
    _____ and _____.
    A. cold; dry   B. cold; damp
    C. hot; damp   D. hot; dry

11. A mass program designed to curb the spread of poliomyeli-   11.___
    tis is based upon hypodermic injection of all children
    under 10 years of age with
    A. blood plasma   B. cortisone
    C. ACTH   D. gamma globulin

12. The one of the following which is a defect of vision is   12.___
    A. aphasia   B. astigmatism
    C. caries   D. toxemia

13. A band of fibrous connective tissue extending from a   13.___
    muscle to a bone is known as a
    A. tendon   B. vein   C. capillary D. nerve

14. The biceps and triceps are the PRINCIPAL muscles of the   14.___
    A. leg   B. chest   C. neck   D. back

15. A cataract is a diseased condition of the   15.___
    A. brain   B. ear   C. eye   D. throat

16. The organ of the body which secretes bile is the   16.___
    A. stomach   B. liver   C. heart   D. kidney

17. Of the following, the one which is NOT a communicable   17.___
    disease is
    A. diabetes   B. diphtheria
    C. smallpox   D. typhoid fever

18. Of the following, the one which is NOT a part of the   18.___
    human skeleton is the
    A. femur   B. humerus   C. tibia   D. brain

19. An opinion as to the probable course and outcome of a   19.___
    disease is known as a(n)
    A. examination   B. diagnosis
    C. case history   D. prognosis

20. Argyrol is MOST commonly associated with treatment of the   20.___
    A. ear   B. eyes   C. mouth   D. nose

21. Of the following, the iron lung is MOST generally used in   21.___
the treatment of
    A. heart disease   B. rheumatic fever
    C. tuberculosis   D. infantile paralysis

22. Post-partum care is GENERALLY given after   22.___
    A. a gall bladder operation
    B. shock therapy
    C. childbirth
    D. an x-ray examination

23. Of the following, the one which is NOT a method of x-ray   23.___
examination is a
    A. pyelogram   B. bronchogram
    C. G.I. series   D. cardiogram

24. The basal metabolism test is used to   24.___
    A. determine the rate at which the body tissues are torn
       down and rebuilt while the patient is at complete
       rest
    B. study the vitamin and mineral needs of the body
    C. determine tendencies toward epileptic attacks under
       alternating conditions of stimulation and rest
    D. study the functioning of the heart at times of
       stress

25. When a person suffers a compound fracture of the leg, IN   25.___
ALL PROBABILITY, the damaged bone is the
    A. radius or ulna   B. clavicle
    C. sternum   D. tibia or fibula

26. Fever, chills, inflamed eyelids, running nose, and cough   26.___
are symptoms of
    A. measles   B. chickenpox
    C. tuberculosis   D. scarlet fever

Questions 27-38.

DIRECTIONS: Column I which follows lists 12 words, numbered 27
                through 38, which are used in medical practice. Column
                II lists phrases which describe the words in Column I.
                In the space at the right, opposite the number pre-
                ceding each of the words in Column I, place the letter
                preceding the phrase in Column II which BEST describes
                the word in Column I.

	COLUMN I		COLUMN II	

27. Antidote

28. Asphyxiation

29. Cathartic

30. Congenital

31. Cyst

32. Fluoroscopy

33. Psychiatry

34. Pulmonary

35. Sedative

36. Subcutaneous

37. Transfusion

38. Vitamins

A. Beneath the skin

B. Examination of the inner parts of the body by use of x-rays and a special screen

C. Relating to the lungs

D. The branch of medicine which specializes in diseases of the mind

E. An abnormal sac containing gas, fluid, or semi-solid matter

F. Medication to counteract poison

G. An instrument used to measure blood pressure

H. Loss of consciousness due to suffocation

I. Resistance to disease

J. Existing at birth

K. Medication used to quiet nerves

L. Abnormal bleeding

M. The transfer of blood from one person to another

N. Chemical substances, present in small amounts in various foods, which are essential to health

O. Purgative or laxative

27.___
28.___
29.___
30.___
31.___
32.___
33.___
34.___
35.___
36.___
37.___
38.___

Questions 39-50.

DIRECTIONS: Column I which follows lists 12 words, numbered 39 through 50, which are used in medical practice. Column II lists phrases which describe the words in Column I. In the space at the right, opposite the number preceding each of the words in Column I, place the letter preceding the phrase in Column II which BEST describes the word in Column I.

COLUMN I	COLUMN II	
39. Antiseptic	A. Expectorated matter, especially mucus	39.___
40. Cardiac		40.___
41. Epidermis	B. A branch of medicine which specializes in the treatment of children	41.___
42. Glaucoma	C. Relating to the heart	42.___
43. Inoculation	D. Breathing	43.___
44. Malignant growth	E. A substance which destroys disease germs	44.___
45. Obesity		45.___
46. Pediatrics	F. The outer layers of the skin	46.___
47. Respiration	G. A disease of the eyeball	47.___
48. Sputum	H. Inflammation of the mucous membrane	48.___
49. Tourniquet	I. Overweight	49.___
50. Wassermann	J. Introduction of the virus of a particular disease into the system through the skin	50.___

K. A blood test for syphilis

L. An instrument used to stop the flow of blood from an artery due to an injury in the arm or leg

M. The collar bone

N. Cancerous tumor which resists treatment and tends to reappear after removal

O. Relating to the kidneys

KEY (CORRECT ANSWERS)

1. B	11. D	21. D	31. E	41. F
2. A	12. B	22. C	32. B	42. G
3. D	13. A	23. D	33. D	43. J
4. A	14. A	24. A	34. C	44. N
5. C	15. C	25. D	35. K	45. I
6. B	16. B	26. A	36. A	46. B
7. A	17. A	27. F	37. M	47. D
8. D	18. D	28. H	38. N	48. A
9. A	19. D	29. O	39. E	49. L
10. C	20. D	30. J	40. C	50. K

TEST 2

DIRECTIONS: Each question or incomplete statement is followed by several suggested answers or completions. Select the one that BEST answers the question or completes the statement. *PRINT THE LETTER OF THE CORRECT ANSWER IN THE SPACE AT THE RIGHT.*

1. Penicillin is effective in the treatment of several   1.____
   diseases because it
   A. builds up bodily resistance to the disease
   B. builds an immunity to the organisms causing the disease
   C. halts the growth of disease-producing organisms
   D. kills the organisms which cause the disease

2. The HIGHEST incidence of tuberculosis occurs during the   2.____
   ages of
   A. 1-9   B. 10-14   C. 15-30   D. 31-45

3. The MOST infectious stage of measles is the   3.____
   A. febrile   B. convalescent
   C. eruptive   D. coryzal

4. When caring for a child ill with measles, you should   4.____
   A. select a room which is light and airy, but you should
      protect the child's eyes from direct light
   B. regulate the temperature of the room to about 72-75°F
   C. keep the child in a darkened room to protect its eyes
   D. have the child wear woolen clothing for warmth

5. Ringworm on the skin is caused by a   5.____
   A. bacterium   B. fungus
   C. protozoan   D. worm

6. Body temperature taken by rectum is _____ body temperature   6.____
   taken orally.
   A. 1° lower than   B. the same as
   C. 1° higher than   D. 2° higher than

7. The dishes used by a patient ill with a communicable   7.____
   disease should be
   A. scraped and rinsed, then washed
   B. soaked overnight in a strong disinfectant solution
   C. boiled for twenty minutes
   D. kept separate and washed with soap and hot water

8. Cold applications tend to   8.____
   A. decrease the supply of blood in the area to which they
      are applied
   B. dilate the blood vessels
   C. bring a greater supply of blood to the area to which
      they are applied
   D. increase the pressure on the nerve endings

9. A bed cradle is a useful device for   9.___
   A. elevating an extremity
   B. keeping the weight of the upper bed covers off the patient
   C. helping to keep a restless patient in bed
   D. allowing for the free circulation of air

10. If a patient shows signs of a pressure sore at the base of   10.___
    the spine, the nurse should
    A. try a sitting position for the patient
    B. use small cotton rings on the pressure spot
    C. apply an ointment to the sore
    D. place an air-ring under the patient's buttocks

11. If a patient lying on her side is uncomfortable, the   11.___
    nurse may give her a(n)
    A. extra top cover
    B. back rest
    C. snug abdominal bandage
    D. pillow to support the lumbar region

12. The diet for a patient with gallstones may include   12.___
    A. grapefruit juice   B. liver
    C. cream   D. peas

13. A rich source of vitamin K is   13.___
    A. butter   B. spinach   C. oranges   D. milk

14. Flaxseed meal is prescribed for making an application of   14.___
    moist heat because of its
    A. medicinal properties   B. mucilaginous ingredients
    C. lightness   D. ability to retain heat

15. Of the following, the substance that is NOT commonly used   15.___
    as an emetic is
    A. bicarbonate of soda   B. mustard powder
    C. syrup of ipecac   D. table salt

16. Supervised practice periods are useful to   16.___
    A. insure continued practice on part of students
    B. prevent wrong bonds from becoming fixed through practice
    C. supplement class instruction
    D. teach children to study

17. The science of human behavior is called   17.___
    A. psychiatry   B. mental hygiene
    C. psychology   D. psychoanalysis

18. The microscopical examination of bacteria is used to   18.___
    determine
    A. best conditions for growth
    B. their virulency
    C. their size, shape, etc.
    D. their relation toward certain foods

19. A disease that confers active immunity is   19.___
    A. scarlet fever   B. erysipelas
    C. pneumonia   D. common colds

20. A serious infection of the eyes is   20.___
    A. trachoma   B. myopia
    C. astigmatism   D. amblyopia

21. A substance that inhibits the growth of bacteria but   21.___
    does NOT destroy them is called
    A. germicide   B. disinfectant
    C. antiseptic   D. sterilizer

22. Organisms which cause diseases of the intestinal tract   22.___
    are
    A. colon bacillus   B. diphtheria bacillus
    C. typhoid bacillus   D. cholera spirillum

23. Proved protection has been discovered against   23.___
    A. smallpox   B. mumps
    C. common colds   D. measles

24. Strabismus is commonly known as   24.___
    A. near-sightedness   B. far-sightedness
    C. cross-eyes   D. pink eyes

25. The country that has the HIGHEST death rate of mothers   25.___
    in childbirth is
    A. England   B. Italy
    C. China   D. United States

Questions 26-40.

DIRECTIONS: Complete the following statements.

26. A birth certificate may be obtained at the Bureau of _____.

27. The vitamin associated with pellagra is _____.

28. The source of insulin is _____.

29. Temporary teeth begin to appear about the age of _____.

30. Bovine tuberculosis affects _____.

31. Quarantine is _____.

32. At the end of the first year, a baby's weight should be _____.

33. An index of the cleanliness of a city's milk supply is determined by _____.

34. The antiscorbutic vitamin is _____.

35. Insulin was discovered by _____.

36. The vitamin associated with polyneuritis is _____.

37. The first permanent molar appears at the age of _____.

38. The separation of persons having communicable disease from others is known as _____.

39. The process of freeing matter from all germ life is _____.

40. Insulin shock is used in the treatment of _____.

Questions 41-50.

DIRECTIONS: Each question consists of a statement. You are to indicate whether the statement is TRUE (T) or FALSE (F).

41. Individuals can be tested for sensitivity to proteins before the injection of certain serums.   41.___

42. The optimum temperature of a schoolroom is 60-65°F.   42.___

43. Certified milk is the best grade of pasteurized milk.   43.___

44. Rickets in children is practically unknown today.   44.___

45. Children have a higher protein requirement proportionally than adults.   45.___

46. Stomatitis is an inflammation of the stomach.   46.___

47. A clean tooth never decays.   47.___

48. The enzyme in the digestive tract which aids in hydroliz- ing fats is steapsin.   48.___

49. All vegetables are good sources of proteins.   49.___

50. The commercial *diaper service* has proved itself safe and satisfactory.   50.___

1. C
2. C
3. D
4. A
5. B

6. C
7. C
8. A
9. B
10. D

11. D
12. A
13. B
14. D
15. A

16. C
17. C
18. C
19. A
20. A

21. B
22. C
23. A
24. C
25. C

26. Records and Statistics, Health Department
27. B complex
28. pancreas
29. 7 months
30. cows (or milkers)

31. the enforced isolation of any person (or place) infected with a contagious disease and his contacts
32. 20 lbs.
33. bacterial counts
34. vitamin C
35. Drs. Banting, Best, and MacLeod in 1921

36. thiamin
37. 6 years
38. isolation
39. sterilization
40. manic depression

41. T
42. T
43. F
44. T
45. T

46. F
47. T
48. F
49. F
50. T

EXAMINATION SECTION
TEST 1

DIRECTIONS: Each question or incomplete statement is followed by several suggested answers or completions. Select the one that BEST answers the question or completes the statement. *PRINT THE LETTER OF THE CORRECT ANSWER IN THE SPACE AT THE RIGHT.*

1. The MOST common cause of death before age 65 is
   A. cerebrovascular disease   B. malignant neoplasm
   C. heart disease   D. diabetes mellitus
   E. liver cirrhosis

   1.___

2. Of the following, the disease NOT transmitted by mosquitoes is
   A. dengue fever
   B. lymphocytic choriomeningitis
   C. western equine encephalitis
   D. St. Louis encephalitis
   E. yellow fever

   2.___

3. The single MOST effective measure to prevent hookworm infection is
   A. washing hands
   B. washing clothes daily
   C. cooking food at high temperatures
   D. wearing shoes
   E. none of the above

   3.___

4. Transmission of tuberculosis in the United States occurs MOST often by
   A. fomites   B. blood transfusion
   C. inhalation of droplet   D. transplacentally
   E. milk

   4.___

5. The second MOST common cause of death in the United States is
   A. accident   B. cancer
   C. cerebrovascular disease   D. heart disease
   E. AIDS

   5.___

6. All of the following bacteria are spread through fecal-oral transmission EXCEPT
   A. haemophilus influenza type B
   B. campylobacter
   C. escherichia coli
   D. salmonella
   E. shigella

   6.___

7. Routine immunization is particularly important for   7.___
   children in day care because preschool-aged children
   currently have the highest age specific incidence of
   all of the following EXCEPT
      A. H-influenzae type B   B. neisseria meningitis
      C. measles   D. rubella
      E. pertussis

8. Hand washing and masks are necessary for physical contact   8.___
   with all of the following patients EXCEPT
      A. lassa fever   B. diphtheria
      C. coxsackie virus disease D. varicella
      E. plaque

9. Control measures for prevention of tick-borne infections   9.___
   include all of the following EXCEPT:
      A. Tick-infested area should be avoided whenever possible.
      B. If a tick-infested area is entered, protective
         clothing that covers the arms, legs, and other exposed
         area should be worn.
      C. Tick/insect repellent should be applied to the skin.
      D. Ticks should be removed promptly.
      E. Daily inspection of pets and removal of ticks is not
         indicated.

10. The PRINCIPAL reservoir of giardia lamblia infection is   10.___
      A. humans   B. mosquitoes   C. rodents
      D. sandflies   E. cats

11. Most community-wide epidemics of giardia lamblia infection   11.___
   result from
      A. inhalation of droplets
      B. eating infected meats
      C. eating contaminated eggs
      D. drinking contaminated water
      E. blood transfusions

12. Epidemics of giardia lamblia occurring in day care centers   12.___
   are USUALLY caused by
      A. inhalation of droplets
      B. person-to-person contact
      C. fecal and oral contact
      D. eating contaminated food
      E. all of the above

13. Measures of the proportion of the population exhibiting   13.___
   a phenomenon at a particular time is called the
      A. incidence   B. prevalence
      C. prospective study   D. cohort study
      E. all of the above

14. The occurrence of an event or characteristic over a   14.___
    period of time is called
        A. incidence   B. prevalence
        C. specificity   D. case control study
        E. cohort study

15. All of the following are live attenuated viral vaccines   15.___
    EXCEPT
        A. measles   B. mumps
        C. rubella   D. rabies
        E. yellow fever

16. Chlorinating air-cooling towers can prevent   16.___
        A. scarlet fever   B. impetigo
        C. typhoid fever   D. mycobacterium tuberculosis
        E. legionnaire's disease

17. Eliminating the disease causing agent may be done by all   17.___
    of the following methods EXCEPT
        A. chemotherapeutic   B. cooling
        C. heating   D. chlorinating
        E. disinfecting

18. Which of the following medications is used to eliminate   18.___
    pharyngeal carriage of neisseria meningitidis?
        A. Penicillin   B. Rifampin
        C. Isoniazid   D. Erythromycin
        E. Gentamicin

19. Post-exposure prophylaxis is recommended for rabies after   19.___
    the bite of all of the following animals EXCEPT
        A. chipmunks   B. skunks   C. raccoons
        D. bats   E. foxes

20. To destroy the spores of clostridium botulinum, canning   20.___
    requires a temperature of AT LEAST _____°C.
        A. 40   B. 60   C. 80   D. 100   E. 120

21. All of the following are killed or fractionated vaccines   21.___
    EXCEPT
        A. hepatitis B   B. yellow fever
        C. H-influenza type B   D. pneumococcus
        E. rabies

22. Of the following, the disease NOT spready by food is   22.___
        A. typhoid fever   B. shigellosis
        C. typhus   D. cholera
        E. legionellosis

23. In the United States, the HIGHEST attack rate of sheigella   23.___
    infection occurs in children between _____ of age.
        A. 1 to 6 months   B. 6 months to 1 year
        C. 1 to 4 years   D. 6 to 10 years
        E. 10 to 15 years

24. Risk factors for cholera include all of the following   24.___
    EXCEPT
    A. occupational exposure
    B. lower socioeconomic
    C. unsanitary condition
    D. high socioeconomic
    E. high population density in low income areas

25. The MOST common cause of traveler's diarrhea is   25.___
    A. escherichia coli   B. shigella
    C. salmonella   D. cholera
    E. campalobacter

KEY (CORRECT ANSWERS)

1. C		11. D	
2. B		12. B	
3. D		13. B	
4. C		14. A	
5. B		15. D	
6. A		16. E	
7. B		17. B	
8. C		18. B	
9. E		19. A	
10. A		20. E	

21. B
22. C
23. C
24. D
25. A

TEST 2

DIRECTIONS: Each question or incomplete statement is followed by several suggested answers or completions. Select the one that BEST answers the question or completes the statement. *PRINT THE LETTER OF THE CORRECT ANSWER IN THE SPACE AT THE RIGHT.*

1. The increased prevalence of entamoeba histolytica   1.___
   infection results from
   A. lower socioeconomic status in endemic area
   B. institutionalized (especially mentally retarded)
      population
   C. immigrants from endemic area
   D. promiscuous homosexual men
   E. all of the above

2. The MOST common infection acquired in the hospital is 2.___
   _____ infection.
   A. surgical wound   B. lower respiratory tract
   C. urinary tract   D. bloodstream
   E. gastrointestinal

3. The etiologic agent of Rocky Mountain spotted fever is 3.___
   A. rickettsia prowazekii   B. rickettsia rickettsii
   C. rickettsia akari   D. coxiella burnetii
   E. rochalimaena quintana

4. The annual death rate for injuries per 100,000 in both 4.___
   sexes is HIGHEST in those _____ years of age.
   A. 1 to 10   B. 10 to 20   C. 30 to 40
   D. 50 to 60   E. 80 to 90

5. The death rate per 100,000 population due to motor   5.___
   vehicle accident is HIGHEST among
   A. whites   B. blacks
   C. Asians   D. native Americans
   E. Spanish surnamed

6. Among the following, the HIGHEST rate of homicide occurs 6.___
   in
   A. whites   B. blacks
   C. native Americans   D. Asians
   E. Spanish surnamed

7. All of the following are true statements regarding   7.___
   coronary heart disease EXCEPT:
   A. About 4.6 million Americans have coronary heart
      disease.
   B. Men have a greater risk of MI and sudden death.
   C. Women have a greater risk of angina pectoris.

D. 25% of coronary heart disease death occurs in individuals under the age of 65 years.
E. White women have a greater risk of MI and sudden death.

8. Major risk factors for coronary heart disease include all of the following EXCEPT
   A. smoking
   B. elevated blood pressure
   C. obesity
   D. high level of serum cholesterol
   E. family history of coronary heart disease
                       8.___

9. The MOST common cancer in American men is
   A. stomach   B. lung   C. leukemia
   D. prostate   E. skin

10. The HIGHEST incidence of prostate cancer occurs in _____ Americans.
   A. white   B. black   C. Chinese
   D. Asian   E. Spanish
                       10.___

11. All of the following are risk factors for cervical cancer EXCEPT
   A. smoking
   B. low socioeconomic condition
   C. first coital experience after age 20
   D. multiple sexual partners
   E. contracting a sexually transmitted disease
                       11.___

12. All of the following are independent adverse prognostic factors for lung cancer EXCEPT
   A. female sex
   B. short duration of symptom
   C. small cell histology
   D. metastatic disease at time of diagnosis
   E. persistently elevated CEA
                       12.___

13. Assuming vaccines with 80% efficacy were available in limited quantity, which vaccine among the following should be given to a military recruit?
   A. Polio   B. Pseudomonas
   C. Meningococcus   D. Influenza
   E. None of the above
                       13.___

14. Among the following, the vaccine which should be administered to children with sickle cell disease is
   A. influenza   B. meningococcus
   C. pseudomonas   D. pneumococcal
   E. yellow fever
                       14.___

15. All of the following are correct statements concerning   15.___
    gastric carcinoma in the United States EXCEPT:
    A. The risk for males is 2.2 times greater than for
       females.
    B. The incidence is increased.
    C. The risk is higher in persons with pernicious anemia
       than for the general population.
    D. City dwellers have an increased risk of stomach
       cancer.
    E. Workers with high levels of exposure to nickle and
       rubber are at increased risk.

16. During the first year of life, a condition that can be   16.___
    detected by screening is
    A. hypothyroidism
    B. RH incompatibility
    C. phenylketonuria
    D. congenital dislocation of the hip
    E. all of the above

17. The major reservoir of the spread of tuberculosis within   17.___
    a hospital is through
    A. patients   B. custodial staff
    C. doctors   D. nursing staff
    E. undiagnosed cases

18. All of the following statements are true regarding tuber-   18.___
    culosis EXCEPT:
    A. Droplet nuclei are the major vehicle for the spread
       of tuberculosis infection.
    B. The highest incidence is among white Americans.
    C. There is a higher incidence of tuberculosis in prison
       than in the general population.
    D. HIV infection is a significant independent risk
       factor for the development of tuberculosis.
    E. A single tubercle bacillus, once having gained access
       to the terminal air spaces, could establish infection.

19. The human papiloma virus is associated with   19.___
    A. kaposi sarcoma
    B. hepatoma
    C. cervical neoplasia
    D. nasopharyngeal carcinoma
    E. none of the above

20. General recommendations for prevention of sexually trans-   20.___
    mitted diseases include all of the following EXCEPT
    A. contact tracing   B. disease reporting
    C. barrier methods   D. prophylactic antibiotic use
    E. patient education

21. Syphilis remains an important sexually transmitted disease because of all of the following EXCEPT its

    A. public health heritage
    B. effect on perinatal morbidity and mortality
    C. association with HIV transmission
    D. escalating rate among black teenagers
    E. inability to be prevented

21.___

22. Which of the following statements about homicide is NOT true?

Approximately

    A. forty percent are committed by friends and acquaintances
    B. twenty percent is committed by spouse
    C. fifteen percent is committed by a member of the victim's family
    D. fifteen percent is committed by strangers
    E. fifteen percent are labeled *relationship unknown*

22.___

23. Conditions for which screening has proven cost-effective include

    A. phenylketonuria   B. iron deficiency anemia
    C. lead poisoning   D. tuberculosis
    E. all of the above

23.___

24. Suicide is MOST common among

    A. whites   B. blacks
    C. hispanics   D. Asians
    E. none of the above

24.___

25. The MOST frequenty used method of suicide is

    A. hanging   B. poisoning by gases
    C. firearms   D. drug overdose
    E. drowning

25.___

KEY (CORRECT ANSWERS)

1. E		11. C	
2. C		12. A	
3. B		13. C	
4. E		14. D	
5. D		15. B	
6. B		16. E	
7. E		17. E	
8. C		18. B	
9. D		19. C	
10. B		20. D	

21. E
22. B
23. E
24. A
25. C

EXAMINATION SECTION

TEST 1

DIRECTIONS: Each question or incomplete statement is followed by several suggested answers or completions. Select the one that BEST answers the question or completes the statement. *PRINT THE LETTER OF THE CORRECT ANSWER IN THE SPACE AT THE RIGHT.*

1. Dichloro-diphenyl-trichloroethane was used MOST effectively as a(n)
   A. disinfectant   B. termite preventative
   C. moth preventative   D. insecticide

1.___

2. Learning by constant repetition without being aware of the thought behind what is being learned is
   A. book learning   B. automation
   C. rationalization   D. rote learning

2.___

3. To cure drug addiction, the A.M.A. believes that the BEST procedure is to
   A. maintain stable dosages in addicts
   B. furnish narcotics at no cost
   C. establish withdrawal clinics
   D. give constant control in a drug-free environment

3.___

4. The purpose of vaccines is to
   A. reduce the causative organism
   B. develop scar tissue
   C. stimulate growth of antibodies
   D. produce bacteriostasis

4.___

5. Of the following, the MOST dangerous of the narcotic poisons is
   A. codeine   B. opium   C. heroin   D. marijuana

5.___

6. If a teenage girl is careless about putting her clothes away,
   A. put the clothing away for her
   B. tolerate the situation
   C. inspire her to be neat
   D. lecture her

6.___

7. A two-year-old child that refuses to eat luncheon should
   A. be forced to eat
   B. be appeased
   C. not be forced to eat, and the food should be removed without comment after a reasonable time has passed
   D. be scolded

7.___

8. Thumbsucking should be eliminated by
   A. satisfying the physical and emotional needs
   B. mechanical restraints
   C. applying distasteful compounds
   D. punishment

8.___

9. During the first three years, the STRONGEST influence on the personality of a child is
    A. his friends
    B. the economic status of the family
    C. the social status of the family
    D. his relationships with his family

9.___

10. For twelve-year-old children, an allowance
    A. may be used as a training device
    B. should be provided
    C. encourages a distorted sense of values
    D. provides a means of disciplinary control

10.___

11. When a child of ten temporarily becomes irritable and boisterous, the parents should
    A. divert his attention   B. punish him
    C. cater to his whims   D. ascertain the reason

11.___

12. Parents should provide opportunities to habituate control of small muscles of the arms when the child
    A. eats solid food
    B. makes an effort to feed himself
    C. eats in restaurants
    D. attends school

12.___

13. Concerning a six-year-old child, parents who insist on absolute perfection may
    A. hamper future accomplishments
    B. encourage good habits
    C. increase mutual love
    D. destroy imitative performance

13.___

14. Lefthandedness
    A. is an individual trait   B. should be corrected
    C. indicates a shortcoming   D. is a conditioned reflex

14.___

15. To reduce fears in children, parents should
    A. give affection   B. lecture them
    C. shield them   D. provide safeguards

15.___

16. When a new baby is expected, to encourage a sense of belonging, older children should be allowed
    A. to anticipate another playmate
    B. no knowledge of the new baby
    C. to know,but not talk,about the new baby
    D. to share in the preparations

16.___

17. First aid care of a third degree burn requires
    A. oil and chalk mixture   B. sterile dressing
    C. antiseptic solution   D. healing ointment

17.___

18. Concerning teeth,
    A. dental caries appear most frequently between ages 12 and 20
    B. dental tartar should not be removed
    C. orthodontia is unimportant
    D. fluorides prevent all decay

18.___

19. Heat destroys bacteria by
    A. enucleation
    B. hemolysis
    C. coagulating protein
    D. making the cell wall permeable

19.___

20. The value of antihistaminic compounds lies PRIMARILY in their ability to
    A. increase intervals between infections
    B. relieve allergic manifestations
    C. immunize
    D. prevent the spread of infection

20.___

21. A test program which gives positive proof of drug addiction is through the use of
    A. hystidine   B. nalline
    C. chlorine   D. choline

21.___

22. Drug withdrawal symptoms in addicts are vomiting and changes in
    A. muscular control   B. nerves
    C. color of the skin   D. pupils of the eyes

22.___

23. The mother of a family should engage in social activities outside the home because they will
    A. prepare her for earning a living should necessity arise
    B. help her to *grow* with her husband
    C. provide a means of solving the children's problems
    D. broaden her own viewpoints and continue development of her own personality

23.___

24. The BEST method of managing family finances is for the breadwinner to
    A. dole out the money when it is needed
    B. turn over all control to the spouse
    C. provide an allowance for each member of the family to use as he pleases
    D. plan cooperatively with the entire family

24.___

25. Non-conforming young children should be
    A. observed and trained while they are young
    B. permitted to outgrow their undesirable traits by themselves
    C. punished at rare intervals
    D. the subject of discussion between members of the family circle without others being present

25.___

26. The home can BEST benefit the mental health of its members through
    A. development of attitudes which result in appropriate emotional expression
    B. an elementary knowledge of psychiatry
    C. a check on the psychosomatics of the older members
    D. regular physical check-ups

26.___

27. When a child expresses fear of darkness on retiring, the BEST procedure is to
    A. make light of his fears
    B. compel him to accept the darkness
    C. provide a dim light
    D. shame him for his fears

    27.____

28. Active immunity is acquired through
    A. production of antibodies
    B. imperviousness of skin tissue
    C. enzyme activity
    D. washing action of mucous membranes

    28.____

29. To avoid detection, the heroin addict injects the
    A. nasal mucosa and the gums
    B. gums and the vagina
    C. nasal mucosa and the vagina
    D. conjunctiva

    29.____

30. A highly dangerous and addictive synthetic narcotic is
    A. amidol   B. amidone   C. cobalamine D. pyridoxine

    30.____

KEY (CORRECT ANSWERS)

1. D	11. D	21. B
2. D	12. B	22. D
3. D	13. A	23. D
4. C	14. A	24. D
5. C	15. A	25. A
6. C	16. D	26. A
7. C	17. B	27. C
8. A	18. A	28. A
9. D	19. C	29. B
10. A	20. B	30. B

TEST 2

DIRECTIONS: Each question or incomplete statement is followed by several suggested answers or completions. Select the one that BEST answers the question or completes the statement. *PRINT THE LETTER OF THE CORRECT ANSWER IN THE SPACE AT THE RIGHT.*

1. Salk serum is administered to prevent   1.___
   A. measles   B. diphtheria
   C. poliomyelitis   D. whooping cough

2. Cancer of the blood is   2.___
   A. carcinoma   B. sarcoma   C. leukemia   D. epithelioma

3. The accepted treatment in severe and extensive radiation burns is to FIRST   3.___
   A. apply tannic acid generously
   B. apply wet sodium bicarbonate dressing
   C. bandage the burned area firmly
   D. put the patient to bed

4. A bed cradle is a device for supporting the   4.___
   A. back   B. knees
   C. bed covering   D. food tray

5. Pediculosis Capitus refers to   5.___
   A. baldness   B. athlete's foot
   C. lice   D. tics

6. The MAIN purpose of a good nursing chart is to   6.___
   A. aid the nurse's memory
   B. help the doctor in diagnosis and treatment
   C. prevent lawsuits
   D. protect the hospital

7. When an ice bag is applied, it should be   7.___
   A. kept filled with ice
   B. strapped in place
   C. removed every 15 or 20 minutes
   D. removed every hour

8. Hepatitis is a disease of the   8.___
   A. renals   B. spleen   C. liver   D. pancreas

9. Bones are joined to one another with   9.___
   A. sinews   B. tendons   C. ligaments   D. membranes

10. Average adult pulse rate for a man is   10.___
    A. 64   B. 72   C. 80   D. 96

11. In MOST cases, to get a doctor in an emergency, call the   11.___
    A. nearest doctor   B. nearest hospital
    C. Red Cross   D. police emergency 911

12. Intravenous injections may be legally administered by the   12.___
    A. registered nurse   B. practical nurse
    C. nursing aide   D. home nurse

13. Persons who are likely to come in contact with communi-   13.___
    cable diseases are immunized by
    A. heredity   B. environment   C. asepsis   D. biotics

14. The temperature of water for a hot water bottle should NOT   14.___
    exceed
    A. 100°F   B. 150°F   C. 125°F   D. 175°F

15. The currently accepted treatment for arthritis is   15.___
    A. x-ray   B. cortisone
    C. aureomycin   D. gold injections

16. The MOST reliable temperature is that found in the   16.___
    A. rectum   B. axilla
    C. mouth   D. none of the above

17. An antiseptic solution recommended in first aid for   17.___
    slight skin scratches (abrasions) is
    A. concentrated boric acid
    B. tincture of merthiolate 1:1000
    C. iodine 2%
    D. tincture of green soap

18. The MOST frequent cause of death in the United States   18.___
    today is
    A. cancer   B. tuberculosis
    C. poliomyelitis   D. heart ailments

19. Average adult temperature by rectum is   19.___
    A. 99.6   B. 97.6   C. 98.6   D. 100.6

20. Metaplasia refers to disturbances of the   20.___
    A. mucous membranes   B. epithelial tissues
    C. cartilage   D. basal metabolism

21. A subjective symptom is one that the patient   21.___
    A. feels   B. hears   C. sees   D. smells

22. A bed cradle   22.___
    A. keeps the patient's weight off the bed
    B. keeps the knees up
    C. elevates the feet
    D. keeps the weight of the covers off the patient

23. Statistics indicate that MOST youngsters start the drug   23.___
    habit with
    A. marijuana   B. heroin   C. cocaine   D. morphine

24. A *stroke* may be caused by   24.___
    A. cerebral hemorrhage   B. caecal dilation
    C. aortal thrombosis   D. pleural edema

25. The control of automatic breathing is located in the   25.___
    A. cerebrum   B. cerebellum
    C. spinal cord   D. medulla oblongata

26. The water for the baby's bath should be   26.___
    A. 90°F   B. 95°F   C. 100°F   D. 105°F

27. The Schick test indicates immunity to   27.___
    A. diphtheria   B. smallpox   C. tetanus   D. tuberculosis

28. Difficulty in speaking is known as   28.___
    A. asphyxia   B. aphasia   C. amnesia   D. anorexia

29. A *water blister* should be   29.___
    A. opened and drained
    B. left unbroken
    C. painted with iodine and bandaged
    D. soaked in hot epsom salt solution

30. The FIRST to be affected by the anesthetizing action of   30.___
    alcohol is the exercise of
    A. judgment   B. memory
    C. muscular coordination   D. control of speech

31. To the nervous system, alcohol acts as a   31.___
    A. depressant   B. stimulant   C. gratifier   D. agitator

32. Acute alcoholism may properly be labeled a psychosis   32.___
    because it involves
    A. intellectual limitations
    B. a loss of contact with reality
    C. emotional inadequacies
    D. bodily disease

33. *Cured* alcoholics   33.___
    A. can control the amount they drink
    B. cannot ever *drink normally*
    C. need moral help to drink within *normal limits*
    D. can drink some alcohol as long as they eat with it

34. Characteristic symptoms of chronic alcoholism include   34.___
    A. exiccosis   B. damage to brain tissue
    C. increase in weight   D. periods of depression

35. Alcohol is MOST often used excessively in order to   35.___
    A. induce sleep
    B. stimulate brain action
    C. overcome social inadequacy
    D. furnish temporary release from tensions

KEY (CORRECT ANSWERS)

1. C	11. D	21. A	31. A
2. C	12. A	22. D	32. B
3. C	13. D	23. A	33. B
4. C	14. C	24. A	34. D
5. C	15. B	25. D	35. D
6. B	16. A	26. C	
7. C	17. C	27. A	
8. C	18. D	28. B	
9. C	19. C	29. B	
10. B	20. C	30. A	

COMMON DIAGNOSTIC NORMS

CONTENTS

COMMON DIAGNOSTIC NORMS

1. RESPIRATION: From 16-20 per minute.

2. PULSE-RATE: Men, about 72 per minute.
    Women, about 80 per minute.

3. BLOOD PRESSURE:
    Men: 110-135 (Systolic)   Women: 95-125 (Systolic)
          70-85 (Diastolic)   65-70 (Diastolic)

4. BASAL METABOLISM: Represents the body energy expended to
    maintain respiration, circulation, etc. Normal rate ranges
    from plus 10 to minus 10.

5. BLOOD:

    a. Red Blood (Erythrocyte) Count:
    Male adult - 5,000,000 per cu. mm.
    Female adult - 4,500,000 per cu. mm.

    (Increased in polycythemia vera, poisoning by carbon monoxide,
    in chronic pulmonary artery sclerosis, and in concentration
    of blood by sweating, vomiting, or diarrhea.)

    (Decreased in pernicious anemia, secondary anemia, and
    hypochronic anemia.)

    b. White Blood (Leukocyte) Count:
    6,000 to 8,000 per cu. mm.

    (Increased with muscular exercise, acute infections,
    intestinal obstruction, coronary thrombosis, leukemias.)

    (Decreased due to injury to source of blood formation and
    interference in delivery of cells to bloodstream, typhoid,
    pernicious anemia, arsenic and benzol poisoning.)

    The total leukocyte group is made up of a number of diverse
    varieties of white blood cells. Not only the total leukocyte
    count, but also the relative count of the diverse varieties,
    is an important aid to diagnosis. In normal blood, from:

    70-72% of the leukocytes are *polymorphonuclear neutrophils*.
    2-4% of the leukocytes are *polymorphonuclear eosinophils*.
    0.5% of the leukocytes are *basophils*.
    20-25% of the leukocytes are *lymphocytes*.
    2-6% of the leukocytes are *monocytes*.

    c. Blood Platelet (Thrombocyte) Count:
    250,000 per cu. mm. Blood platelets are important in blood
    coagulation.

d. Hemoglobin Content:
May normally vary from 85-100%. A 100% hemoglobin content is equivalent to the presence of 15.6 grams of hemoglobin in 100 c.c. of blood.

e. Color Index:
Represents the relative amount of hemoglobin contained in a red blood corpuscle compared with that of a normal individual of the patient's age and sex.

The normal is 1. To determine the color index, the percentage of hemoglobin is divided by the ratio of red cells in the patient's blood to a norm of 5,000,000. Thus, a hemoglobin content of 60% and a red cell count of 4,000,000 (80% of 5,000,000) produces an abnormal color index of .75.

f. Sedimentation Rate:
Represents the measurement of the speed with which red cells settle toward the bottom of a containing vessel. The rate is expressed in millimeters per hour, and indicates the total sedimentation of red blood cells at the end of 60 minutes.

Average rate:	4-7 mm. in 1 hour
Slightly abnormal rate:	8-15 mm. in 1 hour
Moderately abnormal rate:	16-40 mm. in 1 hour
Considerably abnormal rate:	41-80 mm. in 1 hour

(The sedimentation rate is above normal in patients with chronic infections, or in whom there is a disease process involving destruction of tissue, such as coronary thrombosis, etc.)

g. Blood Sugar:
90-120 mg. per 100 c.c. (Normal)
In mild diabetics: 150-300 mg. per 100 c.c.
In severe diabetics: 300-1200 mg. per 100 c.c.

h. Blood Lead:
0.1 mg. or less in 100 c.c. (Normal). Greatly increased in lead poisoning.

i. Non-Protein Nitrogen:
Since the function of the kidneys is to remove from the blood certain of the waste products of cellular activity, any degree of accumulation of these waste products in the blood is a measure of renal malfunction. For testing purposes, the substances chosen for measurement are the nitrogen-containing products of protein combustion, their amounts being estimated in terms of the nitrogen they contain. These substances are urea, uric acid, and creatinine, the sum total of which, in addition to any traces of other waste products, being designated as total non-protein nitrogen (NPN).

The normal limits of NPN in 100 c.c. of blood range from 25-40 mg. Of this total, urea nitrogen normally constitutes 12-15 mg., uric acid 2-4 mg., and creatinine 1-2 mg.

6. URINE:

a. Urine - Lead:
0.08 mg. per liter of urine (normal).
(Increased in lead poisoning.)

b. Sugar:
From none to a faint trace (normal).
From 0.5% upwards (abnormal).
(Increased in diabetes mellitus.)

c. Urea:
Normal excretion ranges from 15-40 grams in 24 hours.
(Increased in fever and toxic states.)

d. Uric Acid:
Normal excretion is variable.
(Increased in leukemia and gout.)

e. Albumin:
Normal renal cells allow a trace of albumin to pass into the urine, but this trace is so minute that it cannot be detected by ordinary tests.

f. Casts:
In some abnormal conditions, the kidney tubules become lined with substances which harden and form a mould or *cast* inside the tubes. These are later washed out by the urine, and may be detected microscopically. They are named either from the substance composing them, or from their appearance. Thus, there are pus casts, epithelial casts from the walls of the tubes, hyaline casts formed from coagulable elements of the blood, etc.

g. Pus Cells:
These are found in the urine in cases of nephritis or other inflammatory conditions of the urinary tract.

h. Epithelial Cells:
These are always present in the urine. Their number is greatly multiplied, however, in inflammatory conditions of the urinary tract.

i. Specific Gravity:
This is the ratio between the weight of a given volume of urine to that of the same volume of water. A normal reading ranges from 1.015 to 1.025. A high specific gravity usually occurs in diabetes mellitus. A low specific gravity is associated with a polyuria.

7. SPINAL FLUID:

    a. Spinal Fluid Pressure (Manometric Reading):
       100-200 mm. of water or 7-15 mm. of mercury (normal).

       (Increased in cerebral edema, cerebral hemorrhage, meningitis, certain brain tumors, or if there is some process blocking the fluid circulation in the spinal column, such as a tumor or herniated nucleus pulposus impinging on the spinal canal.)

    b. Quickenstedt's Sign:
       When the veins in the neck are compressed on one or both sides, there is a rapid rise in the pressure of the cerebrospinal fluid of healthy persons, and this rise quickly disappears when pressure is removed from the neck. But when there is a block of the vertebral canal, the pressure of the cerebrospinal fluid is little or not at all affected by this maneuver.

    c. Cerebrospinal Sugar:
       50-60 mg. per 100 c.c. of spinal fluid (normal).

       (Increased in epidemic encephalitis, diabetes mellitus, and increased intracranial pressure.)

       (Decreased in purulent and tuberculous meningitis.)

    d. Cerebrospinal Protein:
       15-40 mg. per 100 c.c. of spinal fluid (normal).

       (Increased in suppurative meningitis, epileptic seizures, cerebrospinal syphilis, anterior poliomyelitis, brain abscess, and brain tumor.)

    e. Colloidal Gold Test:
       This test is made to determine the presence of cerebrospinal protein.

    f. Cerebrospinal Cell Count:
       0-10 lymphocytes per cu. mm. (normal).

    g. Cerebrospinal Globulin:
       Normally negative. It is positive in various types of meningitis, various types of syphilis of the central nervous system, in poliomyelitis, in brain tumor, and in intracranial hemorrhage.

8. SNELLEN CHART FRACTIONS AS SCHEDULE LOSS DETERMINANTS:

    a. Visual acuity is expressed by a Snell Fraction, where the numerator represents the distance, in feet, between the subject and the test chart, and the denominator represents the distance, in feet, at which a normal eye could read a type size which the abnormal eye can read only at 20 feet.

b. Thus, 20/20 means that an individual placed 20 feet from the test chart clearly sees the size of type that one with normal vision should see at that distance.

c. 20/60 means that an individual placed 20 feet from the test chart can read only a type size, at a distance of 20 feet, which one of normal vision could read at 60 feet.

d. Reduction of a Snellen Fraction to its simplest form roughly indicates the amount of vision remaining in an eye. Thus, a visual acuity of 20/60 corrected implies a useful vision of 1/3 or 33 1/3%, and a visual loss of 2/3 or 66 2/3% of the eye.

Similarly:

Visual Acuity (Corrected)	Percentage Loss of Use of Eye
20/20	No loss
20/25	20%
20/30	33 1/3%
20/40	50%
20/50	60%
20/60	66 2/3%
20/70	70% (app.)
20/80	75%
20/100	100% (since loss of 80% or more constitutes industrial blindness)

ANSWER SHEET

USE THE SPECIAL PENCIL.   MAKE GLOSSY BLACK MARKS.

	A B C D E		A B C D E		A B C D E		A B C D E		A B C D E
1	:: :: :: :: ::	26	:: :: :: :: ::	51	:: :: :: :: ::	76	:: :: :: :: ::	101	:: :: :: :: ::
2	:: :: :: :: ::	27	:: :: :: :: ::	52	:: :: :: :: ::	77	:: :: :: :: ::	102	:: :: :: :: ::
3	:: :: :: :: ::	28	:: :: :: :: ::	53	:: :: :: :: ::	78	:: :: :: :: ::	103	:: :: :: :: ::
4	:: :: :: :: ::	29	:: :: :: :: ::	54	:: :: :: :: ::	79	:: :: :: :: ::	104	:: :: :: :: ::
5	:: :: :: :: ::	30	:: :: :: :: ::	55	:: :: :: :: ::	80	:: :: :: :: ::	105	:: :: :: :: ::
6	:: :: :: :: ::	31	:: :: :: :: ::	56	:: :: :: :: ::	81	:: :: :: :: ::	106	:: :: :: :: ::
7	:: :: :: :: ::	32	:: :: :: :: ::	57	:: :: :: :: ::	82	:: :: :: :: ::	107	:: :: :: :: ::
8	:: :: :: :: ::	33	:: :: :: :: ::	58	:: :: :: :: ::	83	:: :: :: :: ::	108	:: :: :: :: ::
9	:: :: :: :: ::	34	:: :: :: :: ::	59	:: :: :: :: ::	84	:: :: :: :: ::	109	:: :: :: :: ::
10	:: :: :: :: ::	35	:: :: :: :: ::	60	:: :: :: :: ::	85	:: :: :: :: ::	110	:: :: :: :: ::

Make only ONE mark for each answer.   Additional and stray marks may be
counted as mistakes.   In making corrections, erase errors COMPLETELY.

	A B C D E		A B C D E		A B C D E		A B C D E		A B C D E
11	:: :: :: :: ::	36	:: :: :: :: ::	61	:: :: :: :: ::	86	:: :: :: :: ::	111	:: :: :: :: ::
12	:: :: :: :: ::	37	:: :: :: :: ::	62	:: :: :: :: ::	87	:: :: :: :: ::	112	:: :: :: :: ::
13	:: :: :: :: ::	38	:: :: :: :: ::	63	:: :: :: :: ::	88	:: :: :: :: ::	113	:: :: :: :: ::
14	:: :: :: :: ::	39	:: :: :: :: ::	64	:: :: :: :: ::	89	:: :: :: :: ::	114	:: :: :: :: ::
15	:: :: :: :: ::	40	:: :: :: :: ::	65	:: :: :: :: ::	90	:: :: :: :: ::	115	:: :: :: :: ::
16	:: :: :: :: ::	41	:: :: :: :: ::	66	:: :: :: :: ::	91	:: :: :: :: ::	116	:: :: :: :: ::
17	:: :: :: :: ::	42	:: :: :: :: ::	67	:: :: :: :: ::	92	:: :: :: :: ::	117	:: :: :: :: ::
18	:: :: :: :: ::	43	:: :: :: :: ::	68	:: :: :: :: ::	93	:: :: :: :: ::	118	:: :: :: :: ::
19	:: :: :: :: ::	44	:: :: :: :: ::	69	:: :: :: :: ::	94	:: :: :: :: ::	119	:: :: :: :: ::
20	:: :: :: :: ::	45	:: :: :: :: ::	70	:: :: :: :: ::	95	:: :: :: :: ::	120	:: :: :: :: ::
21	:: :: :: :: ::	46	:: :: :: :: ::	71	:: :: :: :: ::	96	:: :: :: :: ::	121	:: :: :: :: ::
22	:: :: :: :: ::	47	:: :: :: :: ::	72	:: :: :: :: ::	97	:: :: :: :: ::	122	:: :: :: :: ::
23	:: :: :: :: ::	48	:: :: :: :: ::	73	:: :: :: :: ::	98	:: :: :: :: ::	123	:: :: :: :: ::
24	:: :: :: :: ::	49	:: :: :: :: ::	74	:: :: :: :: ::	99	:: :: :: :: ::	124	:: :: :: :: ::
25	:: :: :: :: ::	50	:: :: :: :: ::	75	:: :: :: :: ::	100	:: :: :: :: ::	125	:: :: :: :: ::

ANSWER SHEET

TEST NO. _____ PART _____ TITLE OF POSITION _____

PLACE OF EXAMINATION _____ DATE _____

(CITY OR TOWN)   (STATE)

RATING

USE THE SPECIAL PENCIL.   MAKE GLOSSY BLACK MARKS.

	A B C D E		A B C D E		A B C D E		A B C D E		A B C D E
1		26		51		76		101	
2		27		52		77		102	
3		28		53		78		103	
4		29		54		79		104	
5		30		55		80		105	
6		31		56		81		106	
7		32		57		82		107	
8		33		58		83		108	
9		34		59		84		109	
10		35		60		85		110	

Make only ONE mark for each answer.   Additional and stray marks may be
counted as mistakes.   In making corrections, erase errors COMPLETELY.

	A B C D E		A B C D E		A B C D E		A B C D E		A B C D E
11		36		61		86		111	
12		37		62		87		112	
13		38		63		88		113	
14		39		64		89		114	
15		40		65		90		115	
16		41		66		91		116	
17		42		67		92		117	
18		43		68		93		118	
19		44		69		94		119	
20		45		70		95		120	
21		46		71		96		121	
22		47		72		97		122	
23		48		73		98		123	
24		49		74		99		124	
25		50		75		100		125	